HEARERS OF THE
WORD

PRAYING & EXPLORING THE READINGS
LENT & HOLY WEEK: YEAR A

KIERAN J O'MAHONY OSA

Published by Messenger Publications, 2019

ISBN 978 1 78812 118 7

Designed by Messenger Publications Design Department
Cover Images: collage Shutterstock
Typeset in adobe Caslon Pro and Adobe Bitter
Printed by Hussar Books

Messenger Publications,
37 Lower Leeson Street, Dublin D02 W938
www.messenger.ie

In Church

Often I try
To analyse the quality
Of its silences. Is this where God hides
From my searching? I have stopped to listen,
After the few people have gone,
To the air recomposing itself
For vigil. It has waited like this
Since the stones grouped themselves about it.
These are the hard ribs
Of a body that our prayers have failed
To animate. Shadows advance
From their corners to take possession
Of places the light held
For an hour. The bats resume
Their business. The uneasiness of the pews
Ceases. There is no other sound
In the darkness but the sound of a man
Breathing, testing his faith
On emptiness, nailing his questions
One by one to an untenanted cross.

R. S. Thomas

Dedication

For Aidan and Phil O'Mahony

Siblings: children of the same parents,
each of whom is perfectly normal
until they get together.
Sam Levenson

We put in at Syracuse and stayed there three days. From there we cast off and arrived at Rhegium, and after one day a south wind sprang up and on the second day we came to Puteoli. There we found some brothers and were invited to stay with them seven days. And in this way we came to Rome.
(Acts 28:12–14)

Table of Contents

Introduction

What is Lent for? Our English word 'Lent' comes from the verb to lengthen. The days get noticeably longer in the spring and so Lent is an old English word for springtime, a time for new life and fresh growth, a springtime of faith, in the happy phrase of Brother Roger of Taizé.

Lent is an invitation to walk again the journey of renewal and conversion towards our great feasts of Easter and Pentecost. The significance of these days is borne out by the special care given to the choice of readings. The readings can be approached in a variety of ways. On a simple level, the sequence of Gospels is traditional: two scenes from Matthew (the Temptation and the Transfiguration, stories which feature each year), followed by three great symbolic tableaux from the Fourth Gospel (water, light and life). On their own, they would be sufficient to engage us, but there is more.

Each Lent, the lectionary provides a representative sequence of stories from the Old Testament, offering a large narrative arc. In Year A, we hear about the temptation of Adam and Eve in the garden, the call of Abraham to be a universal blessing, Moses striking the rock in the desert, the anointing of David as king over Israel and, finally, a scene from the Exile promising the restoration of Israel using the language of resurrection. The sequence provides a window on the experiences and faith of the people of Israel. Even at a superficial glance, it is evident that the two large narrative arcs, the Old Testament and the Gospel scenes, have been chosen to illuminate each other. In case we should overlook the link, the middle reading functions as bridge – very plain to see on the first and fourth Sundays of Lent, for example. Thus the readings may be approached vertically (from Sunday to Sunday) or horizontally (across all three readings each Sunday).

In a word, the Lent readings form a tapestry, with different narratives stitched together, using overlapping threads and themes. To benefit from this complex arrangement, at the close of each set of notes for Lent, there is an extra reflection, entitled 'Across the Three Readings', to help us engage even more deeply with the word of God.

1	Genesis 2:7-9; 3:1-7	**Adam and Eve**	Romans 5:12-19	**Adam and Jesus**	Matthew 4:1-11	**Temptation in the desert**
2	Genesis 12:1-4	**Abraham**	2 Timothy 1:8-10	**God's grace**	Matthew 17:1-9	**Transfiguration**
3	Exodus 17:3-7	**Moses**	Romans 5:1-2, 5-8	**God's love**	John 4:5-42	**The Samaritan woman**
4	1 Samuel 16:1, 6-7, 10-13	**David**	Ephesians 5:8-14	**Light of Christ**	John 9:1-41	**The Man born blind**
5	Ezekiel 37:12-14	**The Exile**	Romans 8:8-11	**Jesus will give life**	John 11:1-45	**The Raising of Lazarus**

The 'pointers for prayer' in the Gospel notes are almost all by my confrère John Byrne OSA.

Prayer before reading Scripture

Lord, inspire me to read your Scriptures and to meditate upon them day and night. I beg you to give me real understanding of what I read, that I in turn may put its precepts into practice. Yet, I know that understanding and good intentions are worthless, unless rooted in your graceful love. So I ask that the words of Scripture may also be not just signs on a page, but channels of grace into my heart. Amen.

(Origen, AD 184–253)

Chapter 1

Lent, 1A

Thought for the day

The temptations of Jesus are not at all temptations to this or that sin but rather fundamental options that matter for the direction of his life. Jesus was tempted in the course of his ministry to choose other ways of being God's prophet, the Messiah or anointed one. In a less obvious way, we too can be attracted by choices which can shape the way our life unfolds. We ask ourselves, what do I live on? What's my true goal? Where is my nourishment? The human, no less than the Kingdom, is more than food and drink. Only the Word of God truly nourishes and illuminates.

Prayer

Lord, in you we live and move and have our being and we thank you. Help us to place you and your Word at the heart of all we do and, even more, at the core of who we are. Through Christ our Lord. Amen.

Gospel

Mt 4:1 Then Jesus was led up by the Spirit into the wilderness to be tempted by the devil. [2] He fasted forty days and forty nights, and afterwards he was famished. [3] The tempter came and said to him, 'If you are the Son of God, command these stones to become loaves of bread.' [4] But he answered, 'It is written, "One does not live by bread alone, but by every word that comes from the mouth of God."'

Mt 4:5 Then the devil took him to the holy city and placed him on the pinnacle of the temple, ⁶ saying to him, 'If you are the Son of God, throw yourself down; for it is written, "He will command his angels concerning you," and "On their hands they will bear you up, so that you will not dash your foot against a stone."'⁷ Jesus said to him, 'Again it is written, "Do not put the Lord your God to the test."'

Mt 4:8 Again, the devil took him to a very high mountain and showed him all the kingdoms of the world and their splendour; ⁹ and he said to him, 'All these I will give you, if you will fall down and worship me.' ¹⁰ Jesus said to him, 'Away with you, Satan! For it is written, "Worship the Lord your God, and serve only him."' ¹¹ Then the devil left him, and suddenly angels came and waited on him.

Initial observations

The 'Temptation of the Son of God' is found in four documents in the New Testament: in the Synoptic Gospels (Mark 1:12–13, Matthew 4:1–11, Luke 4:1–13) and in Hebrews 2:10–18 and 4:15–16. Mark's account is quite minimal. Matthew and Luke are very alike, although Luke has a different order (bread, mountain, Temple). The temptations are a literary anticipation of the final disputes between Jesus and the Jewish leadership (Matthew 21:23–22:46). The hidden conflict is really God versus Satan. What is at stake throughout is Jesus' vision of the Kingdom of God.

Kind of writing

(i) Commonly in ancient accounts, the 'hero' is tested in some fashion before undertaking his heroic role. The test usually foreshadows realities to follow. It is not, therefore, a story about temptation to this or that moral deviation, but rather a testing of identity and role. Given that Jesus is the Son of God, what *kind* of Son of God will he be?

(ii) Our story resembles the typical manner of 'robust' dispute among rabbis of the period, who often argued by firing texts from Scripture at each other.

(iii) It is a symbolic tale, with a deep, non-literal meaning. (This helps us deal with the impossibility of seeing all of the kingdoms from one mountain and with the mild absurdity of Satan 'whisking' Jesus hither and thither.)

Old Testament background

Often in the New Testament (and especially in Matthew's Gospel), it is helpful to keep an eye on any possible Old Testament background to a particular story or scene. 'The Temptation of the Son of God' is a good example of this. The biblical citations in the story all come from Deuteronomy 6–8. They thus come from that part of the Pentateuch (the first five Books of the Old Testament) where the people of Israel are about to enter the Promised Land after forty years in the desert and Moses reflects on their experience of temptation and failure during that very period.

Even the words used in Matthew reflect Deuteronomy: 'led', 'forty', 'wilderness', 'son of God' (meaning Israel) and 'test'. There is an implied comparison: historical Israel fails the test in the desert and emerges as unfaithful to the covenant, whereas Jesus, the Son of God, comes through successfully and models the fidelity God desires from us. The second background in the Hebrew Bible is, of course, Psalm 91.

Jesus also *recapitulates* the temptations of Israel in the desert: hunger (Exodus 16); testing God (Exodus 17) and idolatry (Exodus 32).

As we read in Psalm 78: *They tested God in their heart by demanding the food they craved. They spoke against God, saying, 'Can God spread a table in the wilderness? Even though he struck the rock so that water gushed out and torrents overflowed, can he also give bread, or provide meat for his people?'* (Psalm 78:18–20)

New Testament foreground

The testing recounted in this Gospel exemplifies challenges faced by Jesus in his ministry. It also anticipates the final testing around the cross. The question of 'what kind of Son of God?' comes back vociferously at the crucifixion.

> Then two bandits were crucified with him, one on his right and one on his left. Those who passed by derided him, shaking their heads and saying, 'You who would destroy the temple and build it in three days, save yourself! If you are the Son of God, come down from the cross.' In the same way the chief priests also, along with the scribes and elders, were mocking him, saying, 'He saved others; he cannot save himself. He is the King of Israel; let him come down from the cross now, and we will believe in him. He trusts in God; let God deliver him now, if he wants to; for he said, "I am God's Son".' The bandits who were crucified with him also taunted him in the same way. (Matthew 27:38–44)

Finally, the sequence in Matthew (different from Luke's) may anticipate a future pattern in this Gospel:
- (i) the multiplication of the breads (Matthew 14:13–21: 'bread').
- (ii) the story of the transfiguration (Matthew 17:1–13: 'tents').
- (iii) the end of the Gospel, on a mountain (Matthew 28:16–20: 'mountain').

St Paul

> So let the one who thinks he is standing be careful that he does not fall. No trial has overtaken you that is not faced by others. And God is faithful: He will not let you be tried beyond what you are able to bear, but with the trial will also provide a way out so that you may be able to endure it. (1 Corinthians 10:12–13)

Guard against self-deception, each of you. If someone among you thinks he is wise in this age, let him become foolish so that he can become wise. For the wisdom of this age is foolishness with God. (1 Corinthians 3:18–19)

Brief commentary

(V. 1)
The desert is more a biblical motif than geography exactly (Deuteronomy 8:2). Being tested was part of Israel's relationship with God — in reality a testing of their fidelity. The wilderness evokes Israel's experience in the wilderness.

(V. 2)
Forty is an evident echo of the years in the desert (Deuteronomy 8:2) and also of the 'heroic' fasts of Moses (Deuteronomy 9:18) and Elijah (1 Kings 19:8). Fasting, as such, was a practice in Matthew's community in Antioch — see Matthew 6:16–18 and 9:14–15.

(V. 3)
The devil is here called the 'tester'. Thus, ironically, the purposes of the Holy Spirit are being fulfilled. 'Son of God' echoes a title of Israel, as a whole, in the Old Testament. The further background here is the story of the manna in the desert. Cf. Psalm 78:18–20 above. Will this Son of God come through the testing? Some Jewish expectations identified the Messiah with a repetition of manna in the desert.

(V. 4)
The quotation comes from Deuteronomy 8:3, where it gives the reason for the manna in the desert. Providing bread for the hungry is also a teaching in Matthew: 6:11; 14:13–21; 15:32–39; 25:31–46.

(V. 5)
The 'holy city' is a rare reference, with messianic overtones. The architectural element is called a 'wing' in Greek, perhaps providing a link with the citation from Psalm 91:4.

(V. 6)

The quotation comes from Psalm 91:11–12. The tempter learns quickly to use Scripture *against* someone for whom it is the Word of God. The launching of textual 'missiles' would have been familiar from rabbinic debates.

(V. 7)

Jesus' response comes from Deuteronomy 6:16. Again, in the background lies Israel's (failed) testing in the desert (cf. Matthew 26:36–53).

(V. 8)

'To a very high mountain' is added by Matthew and underlines the link with Moses. Again, although some echo of Moses' panoramic view of the Holy Land may be intended (Deuteronomy 34:1–4), it is not geography that counts. For the real mountain of authority, see Matthew 28:18.

(V. 9)

'Homage' to Jesus himself frames this whole Gospel, from the Magi to the disciples on the mountain in chapter 28.

(V. 10)

Away with you, Satan! A very interesting phrase, which Matthew alone places here, thus making a dramatic link with the same phrase (Matthew 16:23), when Peter misunderstands radically the kind of Messiah Jesus intended to be: (lit.) *Away with you, behind me, Satan!*

(V. 11)

'Angels' indicate obliquely that some experience of the transcendent took place. Cf. Matthew 28:2.

Pointers for prayer

a) In today's gospel Jesus is enticed to gratify his own needs, or to perform some spectacular act in public. He rejects the temptation because he chooses commitment to his mission and dependence on his Father over any immediate gratification. We can all be tempted to go for some immediate satisfaction ... but is that where true happiness lies? Have you found that sometimes it can be more life-giving to say 'no' to your immediate desires for the sake of some long-term goal? What are the goals, aims and values that inspire you in this way?

b) One way of looking at this gospel is to say that Jesus went into the desert to face his demons. We all have demons we need to face — compulsions, fears, prejudices, anger and urges that lurk within. It is in facing our demons that we find a way to live a fuller life. Can you recall a time when you grew through facing a 'demon' in this way?

Prayer

Lord our God, in every age you call a people to hear your word and to do your will.

Renew us in these Lenten days: washed clean of sin, sealed with the Spirit and sustained by your living bread, may we remain true to our calling and, with the elect, serve you alone.

We make our prayer through our Lord Jesus Christ, our liberator from sin, who lives and reigns with you in the unity of the Holy Spirit, holy and mighty God for ever and ever. Amen.

🌿 Second Reading 🌿

Rom 5:12 So then, just as sin entered the world through one man and death through sin, and so death spread to all people because all sinned – [13] for before the law was given, sin was in the world, but there is no accounting for sin when there is no law. [14] Yet death reigned from Adam until Moses even over those who did not sin in the same way that Adam (who is a type of the coming one) transgressed. [15] But the gracious gift is not like the transgression. For if the many died through the transgression of the one man, how much more did the grace of God and the gift by the grace of the one man Jesus Christ multiply to the many! [16] And the gift is not like the one who sinned. For judgement, resulting from the one transgression, led to condemnation, but the gracious gift from the many failures led to justification. [17] For if, by the transgression of the one man, death reigned through the one, how much more will those who receive the abundance of grace and of the gift of righteousness reign in life through the one, Jesus Christ!

Rom 5:18 Consequently, just as condemnation for all people came through one transgression, so too through the one righteous act came righteousness leading to life for all people. [19] For just as through the disobedience of the one man many were made sinners, so also through the obedience of one man many will be made righteous.

Initial observations

Our reading, though challenging, is quite appropriate for the start of Lent and especially in the light of the first reading from Genesis.

Kind of writing

In Romans 1–4, Paul deconstructs any superiority or boasting by pointing out that both sides (see below) are equally adept at sinning and both sides stand in need of grace and faith. In Romans 5–8, Paul again deconstructs attitudes of superiority, but this time by pointing out how much they both share indistinguishably in Christ. The gifts are listed chronologically: faith and salvation (5), baptism (6), the moral struggle (7) and the capacity to call God 'Abba' by the power of the Holy Spirit and our unshakeable hope in Christ (8). In Romans 5, Adam is summoned up to show the universality of grace in Christ. The *sin* of Adam is evoked to underline the *contrast* between Adam's sin and the grace of Christ ('all the more so'). The comparison of the beginning, Adam, and the end, Christ (protology and eschatology) is typically

Apocalyptic. Such patterning underscores purpose, even when the end (grace) so far outstrips the beginning (sin). Cf. 1 Corinthians 15:21–23, 45–49 below.

NB: In Romans 5:12–19, Paul interrupts himself. The thought in v. 12 is suspended and resumed eventually only in v. 18. The long suspension of vv. 13–17 makes the passage hard to grasp as Paul considers first sin, death and the Law, and then grace, justification and life. Cf. Galatians 3.

Context in the community

The letter to the Romans is big in every sense. Nevertheless, the persuasive outline is relatively clear. The context is division in the Roman house churches between disciples of Jewish and Gentile backgrounds. The issue at stake resembles the issue in Galatians: how much of the Jewish Law should be retained and followed? It is evident from the letter that the community itself is divided into the 'weak' and the 'strong'. Who these are becomes clear only in the final section, 12:1–15:6. However, in 1:16–4:23 and in chapters 9–11, it is evident that each side looks down upon the other (the word despise is used). Such a division in the capital is harmful and goes clean against Paul's vision of the union of Jew and Gentile in Christ crucified and risen.

Related passages

For since death came through a man, the resurrection of the dead also came through a man. For just as in Adam all die, so also in Christ all will be made alive. But each in his own order: Christ, the first fruits; then when Christ comes, those who belong to him. (1 Corinthians 15:21–23)

So also it is written, 'The first man, Adam, became a living person'; the last Adam became a life-giving spirit. However, the spiritual did not come first, but the natural, and then the spiritual. The first man is from the earth, made of dust; the second man is from heaven. Like the one made of dust, so too are those made of dust, and like the one from heaven, so too those who are heavenly. And just as we have borne the image of the man of dust, let us also bear the image of the man of heaven. (1 Corinthians 15:45–49)

Brief commentary

(V. 12)

Both sin and death are universal – not because Adam sinned but because all have sinned (*pace* Augustine!).

(V. 13)

Even though there was no law forbidding transgression there was sin – a kind of spiritual force, causing death. Cf. Galatians 3:19–29.

(V. 14)

Death (and hence sin) reigned in the time between Adam and Moses, that is, even when there was no Torah.

(V. 15)

The second Adam resembles the first *in terms of universality*. They differ strikingly *in the quality of their effects*: grace far, far surpasses transgression. Paul's *style* is 'all the more so', and the *content* is the astonishing gracious gift, repeatedly affirmed and insisted upon.

(V. 16)

Although Adam and Christ resemble each other in function, the difference is greater still: after *one* sin came judgement, after *many* transgressions came justification ('right relationship'). Congruence takes you only so far.

(V. 17)

The contrast continues in the consequences: death versus abundance of grace, gift of righteousness ('right relationship') and life. The 'how much more' approach places all the emphasis on our new situation in Christ.

(V. 18)

At last, v. 12 is resumed: the universality of need (illustrated in sin and death) is matched by the universality of grace (righteousness and life) in Christ. 'Obedience' refers to Jesus' faithfulness – cf. Romans 3:21–26.

(V. 19)

A final and, we may hope, relatively plain summary of vv. 12–18.

Pointers for prayer

a) The abundance of grace: When did I become aware God's greater love?

b) All of us are put into right relationship – a pure gift, received in gratitude.

Prayer

Loving and ever faithful God, no words of ours can express the depth of your gifts of grace and life in Christ, so loving, so free, so abundant. May our gratitude be expressed in our lives. Through Christ our Lord. Amen.

🌿 First Reading 🌿

Gen 2:7 Then the Lord God formed man from the dust of the ground, and breathed into his nostrils the breath of life; and the man became a living being. [8] And the Lord God planted a garden in Eden, in the east; and there he put the man whom he had formed. [9] Out of the ground the Lord God made to grow every tree that is pleasant to the sight and good for food, the tree of life also in the midst of the garden, and the tree of the knowledge of good and evil.

Gen 3:1 Now the serpent was more crafty than any other wild animal that the Lord God had made. He said to the woman, 'Did God say, "You shall not eat from any tree in the garden"?' [2] The woman said to the serpent, 'We may eat of the fruit of the trees in the garden; ³ but God said, 'You shall not eat of the fruit of the tree that is in the middle of the garden, nor shall you touch it, or you shall die.' ⁴ But the serpent said to the woman, 'You will not die; ⁵ for God knows that when you eat of it your eyes will be opened, and you will be like God, knowing good and evil.' ⁶ So when the woman saw that the tree was good for food, and that it was a delight to the eyes, and that the tree was to be desired to make one wise, she took of its fruit and ate; and she also gave some to her husband, who was with her, and he ate. ⁷ Then the eyes of both were opened, and they knew that they were naked; and they sewed fig leaves together and made loincloths for themselves.

Initial observations

Before taking on this reading, cast an eye over the chart in the introduction. Lent this year offers the traditional sequence of gospels as well as a large narrative arc in the Old Testament readings. Lent, Holy Week and the Easter Triduum are enriched by substantial biblical catechesis and the spine of this catechesis is the great narrative of the Hebrew Bible, taking us from Adam to the exile in Babylon. In Lent, the link with the Gospel may not be initially evident. Even so, on each Sunday we find themes shared across all three readings.

Kind of writing

Technically, this is an etiological tale, a story that accounts for why things are the way they are. Such 'explorations' abound in Genesis.

Origin of the reading

The reading comes from the Book of Genesis; more precisely, it comes from the so-called Prehistory, from creation to the tower of Babel (a very different sequence begins with the call of Abram in chapter 12). In terms of sources, our text belongs to the Yahwist source of the Pentateuch (using YHWH for God). The Yahwist always writes engagingly and very naturally, being totally unafraid to portray God in a touchingly human way.

Related passages

There are other creation stories in the Bible and not just the two that are familiar from Genesis. The Jewish tradition is never afraid to look at the same reality from widely differing perspectives. Here is an approximate list: Genesis 1:1–2:4a (the Priestly account; see also Psalm 104); Psalms 65:6–7; 74:12–17; 89:9–14; Job 9:5–14; 26:5–15; 38–39; Ezekiel 28:11–19 and many references in Second Isaiah (40–55).

Brief commentary

(V. 2:7)

In a very plastic way, God shapes the human (= *'adam*) from the soil (= *'adamah*). This image of the creator as a potter was widespread in the ancient Near East. In this account, humans are of lowlier origin than in 1:26–28, being moulded from the soil; yet there is greater intimacy with the creator in the Yahwist account. Cf. Job 10:9: *Remember that you fashioned me like clay; and will you turn me to dust again?*

(V. 8)

Eden is found a few times in the Bible: Genesis 2:8,10,15; 3:23–24; 4:16; Isaiah 51:3; Ezekiel 28:13; 31:9, 16, 18; 36:35; Joel 2:3. The garden of YHWH is mentioned twice: Genesis 13:10; Isaiah 51:3. The Greek translates garden as *paradeisos* (a Persian loan word, indicating a pleasure park), whence our word paradise. The original Hebrew — simply a *garden* in Eden — has no particular connotation of pleasure.

(V. 9)

Note that there are different kinds of trees in Eden. The tree of life is mentioned first and then ignored. The tree of knowledge becomes immediately more significant. 'Good and evil' may be a *merism*, a figure of speech in which opposing realities denote the totality of something as such. Hence, the tree of knowledge *of everything*.

(V. 3:1)

Crafty (= *'arum*) is a play of words on naked (= *'arumim*) in the preceding verse: *And the man and his wife were both naked* (Genesis 2:25). As for the snake, cf. *On that day the* LORD *with his cruel and great and strong sword will punish Leviathan the fleeing serpent, Leviathan the twisting serpent, and he will kill the dragon that is in the sea* (Isaiah 27:1).

(V. 2)

Responding, the woman unfolds the ground rules for living in Eden.

(V. 3)

Notice that Eve expands the original prohibition to include even touching the tree. There is a Talmudic dictum: *whoever adds to a commandment subtracts from it!*

(V. 4)

The serpent contradicts God and, in a way, correctly, for Adam and Eve do not die *immediately* upon eating the fruit but only later.

(V. 5)

The serpent 'explains' that God acted out of jealousy, thus impugning God's motives. Note the contrast with Genesis 1: there, humans are God-like as a gift, but here they aspire to being God-like, as a sinful ambition. Eve's 'progress' to sin is a climax: from the physical (eating), through the aesthetic (the eyes) to the intellectual (knowledge).

(V. 6)

Delight is quite strong in Hebrew, indicating desire, appetite and sometimes even lust. 'To make one wise': early translations have 'to look at'; perhaps both meanings are intended. Seeing and knowing are often linked in the Bible. Very quickly, the deed is done: Eve succumbs and Adam sins.

(V. 7)

As the serpent correctly predicted, their eyes were indeed opened. Shame captures the consequent ambiguity of the achievement.

Pointers for prayer

a) Each of us comes from the hands of God, who shapes us as a potter shapes the clay. We are in his hands.

b) Genesis 2–3 is often understood as the story of any human being *in nuce*, as we move from innocence, to awareness, to transgression and to responsibility. Can I see myself in the story, as my life has unfolded and evolved?

Prayer

God, we are the clay, you are the potter. You put before us life and death: help us by your grace to choose life again and again. Through Christ our Lord. Amen.

Themes across the readings

Genesis as a 'story of origins' is really the life of every human being, as we each move from innocence to knowledge and transgression, as we grow from being alone to seeking companionship, as we learn to leave behind the security of childhood to accepting work, hardship, responsibilities and even death itself. Biblically, the story is really about us.

The second reading also reflects on origins but — and this is vital to Paul's argument — from the perspective of faith in Christ. In Romans 5–8, Paul is outlining all the wonderful gifts that unite us in Christ: salvation, faith, baptism, the Holy Spirit, unshakeable love in Christ and so forth. On the way, he names our need for such great gifts: it is the human condition (going back symbolically to Adam in Romans 5) and it is the existential reality of each one (as we see in Romans 7). But all in the light of God's victory in Christ. Paul moves from the cure, so to speak, to the disease, from Christ back to Adam. Only in the light of grace is our need truly apparent. That is why Romans 5 begins on such a positive note; in fact all of Romans 5–8 is found *in nuce* in the very first five verses.

Finally, in the account of the temptations, Jesus himself illustrates the human condition of inclination to distorted options and the imposed freedom of having no choice but to choose. Naturally, we are only at the beginning of the ministry; the true battle over evil is at the end of that ministry, on the cross and in the resurrection.

Chapter 2

Lent 2A

Thought for the day

Every so often, we catch a glimpse of the 'something more' that God has in store for us. These fleeting experiences are to be treasured: the birth of my first child, falling in love, a sense of 'being held' by God's presence. Such experiences may help us approach the Transfiguration. Like all transcendent experiences, it is fleeting, yet it etches a memory and leaves a longing. What should we do? Practise listening to him. Be not afraid. We cannot always be 'on the mountain', yet what happens on the heights can help us on the lowlands of the everyday.

Prayer

Lord, listening sounds so easy and yet is such hard work! Guide us as we listen to your Son, whose word is alive, who is himself the way, the truth and the life. Through Christ our Lord. Amen.

🌿 Gospel 🌿

Mt 17:1 Six days later, Jesus took with him Peter and James and his brother John and led them up a high mountain, by themselves. ² And he was transfigured before them, and his face shone like the sun, and his clothes became dazzling white. ³ Suddenly there appeared to them Moses and Elijah, talking with him. ⁴ Then Peter said to Jesus, 'Lord, it is good for us to be here; if you wish, I will make three dwellings here, one for you, one for Moses, and one for Elijah.' [5] While he was still speaking, suddenly a bright cloud overshadowed them, and from the cloud a voice said, 'This is my Son, the Beloved; with him I am well pleased; listen to him!' [6] When the disciples heard this, they fell to the ground and were overcome by fear. [7] But Jesus came and touched them, saying, 'Get up and do not be afraid.' [8] And when they looked up, they saw no one except Jesus himself alone.

Mt 17:9 As they were coming down the mountain, Jesus ordered them, 'Tell no one about the vision until after the Son of Man has been raised from the dead.'

Initial observations

The account of the Transfiguration can be found in Mark 9:2–8, Luke 9:28–36 and here in Matthew. It is also mentioned in 2 Peter 1:16–18. The Transfiguration account recalls the Baptism of Jesus and, in a way, looks forward to the prayer in Gethsemane. In this Gospel, Peter has just made a profound confession of faith (16:16), so he is 'on the right track.' Nevertheless, the place of suffering in the identity of Jesus as Messiah still continues to elude him. The continuation of the story in vv. 10–23 is essential for our appreciation of what Matthew is trying to teach here.

Kind of writing

This is an 'epiphany', an appearance or revelation of a divine person. Matthew, Mark and Luke all tell the same basic story, which is one of transformation in prayer, a mystical moment, in which some of the disciples are involved. It bridges the time between the baptism and the resurrection.

After that basic account, each writer shapes the story for his own particular goals. In Mark, it is to encourage the disciples on the way of the cross. In Luke, it is a moment of prayer, marking the departure of Moses and Elijah.

Our Gospel, Matthew, invests the story with apocalyptic language (*transfigured, face shone like the sun, dazzling white, touched*), thus letting the reader know that Jesus is of ultimate significance in God's plan for human history and so also for us.

Matthew recounts the Transfiguration as an apocalyptic vision, one of those 'moments' of transcendence and transformation, never to be forgotten. The concentric pattern tells us that the centre is v. 5, that the divine voice is given a central role.

a. Narrative introduction (v. 1)
b. Jesus is transfigured (vv. 2–3)
c. Peter's response (v .4)
d. *The divine voice* (v. 5)
c*. The disciples' response (v. 6)
b*. Jesus speaks (v. 7)
a*. Narrative conclusion (v. 8)

x. Postlude (v. 9)

Old Testament background

There are four Old Testament texts to keep in mind. Deuteronomy 18:15 promises a prophet *like* Moses at the end. Malachi 4:5 predicts that Elijah will have a role ushering in the end of time. Most important are the passages from Exodus and the prophet Daniel.

> (i) Then Moses *went up* on the *mountain*, and the *cloud covered the mountain*. The glory of the Lord settled on Mount Sinai, and the *cloud covered it for six days*; on the seventh day he called to Moses *out of the cloud*. Now the *appearance* of the glory of the Lord was like a devouring fire on the top of the *mountain* in the sight of the people of Israel. Moses entered the cloud, and *went up on the mountain*. Moses was on the mountain for forty days and forty nights. (Exodus 24:15–18)

> (ii) Moses *came down* from Mount Sinai. As he *came down from the mountain* with the two tablets of the covenant in

his hand, Moses did not know that the skin of *his face shone* because he had been talking with God. When Aaron and all the Israelites saw Moses, the skin of his *face was shining*, and *they were afraid* to come near him. (Exodus 34:29–30)

(iii) So he came near where I stood; and when he came, I became *frightened* and fell *prostrate*. But he said to me, 'Understand, O mortal, that the *vision* is for the time of the end.' As he was speaking to me, I *fell* into a trance, face to the ground; then he *touched* me and set me on my feet. (Daniel 8:17–18)

(iv) I, Daniel, alone saw the *vision*; the people who were with me did not see the vision, though a great trembling fell upon them, and they fled and hid themselves. So I was left alone to see this great *vision*. My strength left me, and my complexion grew deathly pale, and I retained no strength. Then I heard the *sound of his words*; and when I heard the *sound of his words*, I *fell* into a trance, face to the ground. But then a hand *touched me* and roused me to my hands and knees. (Daniel 10:7–10)

New Testament foreground

This story echoes in the ministry the baptism of Jesus and marks some kind of appropriation of what happened then. The resurrection is in our minds as well, because of the dazzling white garments and the explicit mention at the end. Matthew wrote for a Jewish-Christian community and portrays Jesus as a Moses-type figure (in this Gospel, John the Baptist is identified as the latter-day Elijah). Jesus has just been talking about his death and Peter has quite spontaneously rejected the cross.

St Paul

It is necessary to boast; nothing is to be gained by it, but I will go on to visions and revelations of the Lord. I know a person in Christ who fourteen years ago was caught up to the third heaven — whether in the body or out of the body I do not know; God knows. And I know that such a person — whether in the body or out of the body I do not know; God knows — was caught up into Paradise and heard things that are not to be told, that no mortal is permitted to repeat. On behalf of such a one I will boast, but on my own behalf I will not boast, except of my weaknesses. But if I wish to boast, I will not be a fool, for I will be speaking the truth. But I refrain from it, so that no one may think better of me than what is seen in me or heard from me, even considering the exceptional character of the revelations. (2 Corinthians 12:1–7)

Brief commentary

(V. 1)
The number 'six' comes from the Exodus account above; Peter, James and John feature together in the Gospels (call, Transfiguration, discipleship dispute, Gethsemane). No purpose is given for the journey (unlike in Luke). The mountain is the symbolic place of encounter with God, especially in the Mosaic traditions.

(V. 2)
'Transfigured': this is difficult to interpret – some kind of glimpse of the future, Risen Lord. 'Like the sun': cf. Revelation 1:16 and Matthew 13:43. 'Dazzling white': see Matthew 28:3. These symbolic details tell us Jesus entered the transcendent world of God. Cf. 'And all of us, with unveiled faces, seeing the glory of the Lord as though reflected in a mirror, are being transformed into the same image from one degree of glory to another; for this comes from the Lord, the Spirit.' (2 Corinthians 3:18)

(V. 3)
Moses and Elijah represent the Law and the Prophets, and thus are symbolic of continuity and fulfilment. In Jewish tradition, the end of time was to be marked by their return.

(V. 4)

Jesus is called 'Lord', not 'rabbi' as in Mark, because Peter believes. The experience is wonderful and Peter wishes to hold on to it. 'Tents' hints at the feast of Succoth/Tabernacles. Peter apparently thinks the figures are equal, a misunderstanding corrected in v. 5.

(V. 5)

Bright cloud: a kind of oxymoron expressing mystery and transcendence (that is, God is present elusively). The words are identical at the baptism (Matthew 3:17), with the addition 'Listen to him!'. They hint at other Old Testament resonances: Messiah (Psalm 2:7), beloved son (Isaac, Genesis 22:2) and the Suffering Servant (Isaiah 42:1; 44:2).

(V. 6)

Not *psychological* fear, but existential dread or awe before the mystery.

(V. 7)

Everybody who is anybody in the Bible is told not to be afraid! Jesus *touches* them — a detail only in Matthew and reminding us of Daniel's visions.

(V. 8)

Suddenly, the experience is over. The real, lasting glory of Jesus follows on the cross and in the resurrection.

(V. 9)

Matthew alone calls it a 'vision'. This verse makes the important connection with the resurrection.

Pointers for prayer

a) The transfiguration experience was one that, for Jesus, clarified his relationship with his Father and strengthened him for the future. What have been the experiences, the moments of insight, that have clarified your sense of who you are, and what your relationship with God is?

b) On the mountain the disciples saw Jesus in a new way.

Sometimes in friendship there are moments of sharing in which we get to know a friend in a new and deeper way. Have you had that experience in human friendship, or in your relationship with Jesus and God? Recall when that happened, and what it was like for you.

c) The clear vision of Jesus with Moses and Elijah was followed by a frightening experience of being in a cloud, and it was in the midst of the cloud that the disciples were instructed 'This is my Son, the Beloved; listen to him'. Have you had the experience of learning the truth about life and about your relationship with God from moments of confusion as well as from times of special joy?

d) After their special experience the disciples came down the mountain again. We cannot live each day at the level of special spiritual experiences, but the memory of them can strengthen us in difficult times. What memories encourage you in time of trouble?

Prayer

Holy God, from the dazzling cloud you revealed Jesus in glory as your beloved Son.

During these forty days, enlighten your Church with the bright glory of your presence.

Inspire us by your word, and so transform us into the image of the risen Lord, who lives and reigns with you in the unity of the Holy Spirit, holy and mighty God for ever and ever. Amen.

🍃 Second Reading 🍃

2 Tim 1:3 I am thankful to God, whom I have served with a clear conscience as my ancestors did, when I remember you in my prayers as I do constantly night and day. ⁴ As I remember your tears, I long to see you, so that I may be filled with joy. ⁵ I recall your sincere faith that was alive first in your grandmother Lois and in your mother Eunice, and I am sure is in you.

2 Tim 1:6 Because of this I remind you to rekindle God's gift that you possess through the laying on of my hands. [7] For God did not give us a Spirit of fear but of power and love and self-control.

2 Tim 1:8 So do not be ashamed of the testimony about our Lord or of me, a prisoner for his sake, but by God's power accept your share of suffering for the gospel. [9] He is the one who saved us and called us with a holy calling, not based on our works but on his own purpose and grace, granted to us in Christ Jesus before time began, [10] but now made visible through the appearing (*epiphaneia*) of our Saviour Christ Jesus. He has broken the power of death and brought life and immortality to light through the gospel!

Initial observations

Our reading from 2 Timothy is chosen for three reasons: (i) the word 'appearing' (*epiphaneia*) makes a link with the Transfiguration; (ii) suffering reminds us of Lent and the passion of Jesus; (iii) the resurrection is richly proclaimed.

Kind of writing

Verses	Sequence
1:1-2	Greeting
1:3-14	Thanksgiving
1:15-18	A personal note
2:1-4:8	Body of the letter
4:9-22	Personal note and prayer

Like 1 Timothy, 2 Timothy is most likely written in the name of Paul to a later, probably third generation of believers. Within the letter, Paul is portrayed as an old man in prison and the letter is in the genre of last

will and testament, a type of writing familiar from the period. Compare: Genesis 49 (Jacob); Deuteronomy 31 (Moses); Joshua 24 (Joshua), John 14–16 (Jesus); Acts 20:18–38 (Paul).

Our reading is the central section of the thanksgiving. Vv. 9–10 are in poetic, balanced, antithetical form.

Context in the community

The issue behind 2 Timothy is a frequent one in intentional communities: how to manage after the departure of the founder/mentor/genius. Accordingly, the letter has a valedictory tone. At the same time, there is a message of consolation for the present moment.

Related passages

Share in *suffering* like a good soldier of Christ Jesus. No one serving in the army gets entangled in everyday affairs; the soldier's aim is to please the enlisting officer. In the case of an athlete, no one is crowned without competing according to the rules. It is the farmer who does the work who ought to have the first share of the crops. (2 Timothy 2:3–6)

I solemnly charge you before God and Christ Jesus, who is going to judge the living and the dead, and by his appearing (*epiphaneia*) and his kingdom: Preach the message, be ready whether it is convenient or not, reprove, rebuke, exhort with complete patience and instruction. (2 Timothy 4:1–2)

Finally the crown of righteousness is reserved for me. The Lord, the righteous Judge, will award it to me in that day — and not to me only, but also to all who have set their affection on his appearing (*epiphaneia*). (2 Timothy 4:8)

The lofty–minded youth, a true son of Abraham, did not groan, but as though transformed in the fire into *immortality*, he nobly endured the torments. (4 Maccabees 9:21–22)

Victory meant *incorruptibility* in long–lasting life. (4 Maccabees 17:12b)

Brief commentary

(V. 8)

The rekindling of charism takes in the capacity to suffer for the Gospel, after the example of Paul. Only here in the Pastorals is Paul called a prisoner (cf. Ephesians 3:1; 4:1; Philemon 1, 9). 'To suffer with' is distinctive of 2 Timothy. See 2 Timothy 2:3, 11–12. Conflict with the culture is to be expected, if the proclamation is genuine. 'Not to be ashamed' reminds us that the cross was, of course, shameful and scandalous.

(V. 9)

The next two verses offer a rich summary of the Gospel proclamation. God, in the Pastorals, offers to all of humanity the gift of salvation. See 1 Tim 2:4, 6:12. Those who believe are called by God's election, echoing the prophetic calls of old. The Pastorals often urge the readers to do good works, with many practical examples. Nevertheless, such effort is not the *source* of salvation but rather a *living out* of the grace already received. It is all God's work, as his purpose and grace are disclosed (2 Corinthians 5:18). All of this has a cosmic dimension, being prepared before time began. Owing everything to God's grace/favour is very strong in the Pastorals as a whole: 1 Timothy 1:2, 12, 14; 6:21; 2 Timothy 1:2–3, 9; 2:1; 4:22; Titus 1:4; 2:11; 3:7, 15.

(V. 10)

'Made visible' is a good translation, because the appearance points to the historical Jesus' mission. Thus, while the emphasis in the pastorals is on Jesus' saving death and resurrection, the incarnation and ministry are not overlooked. In plain language, Jesus has broken the power of death. Cf. the Pauline teaching in 1 Corinthians 15:26 and 54. Life here is really life in the new creation at the end of time, eschatological life. The writer adds the expression 'immortality' (lit. imperishability), which is not a Hebrew concept but one taken from the surrounding culture. However, see Wisdom 2:23, 6:19 and 4 Maccabees 9:22 and 17:12 (these latter two cited above for convenience). This offer of salvation is made to all through the proclamation of the Good News.

Pointers for prayer

a) Any generation could feel ashamed of the Gospel — perhaps a special risk today. When have I borne witness?

b) Our riches in Christ: what does it mean *to me* to be saved and called through the Gospel?

c) The sense of grace and gift is strong here. Recall your own sense of being favoured and unexpectedly graced.

Prayer

As we remember in these days the great events that gave us new life in Christ, renew our faith in him, who broke the power of death and brought us life and immortality. He lives for ever and ever! Amen.

🌿 First Reading 🌿

Gen 11:27 Now these are the descendants of Terah. Terah was the father of Abram, Nahor and Haran; and Haran was the father of Lot. ²⁸ Haran died before his father Terah in the land of his birth, in Ur of the Chaldeans. ²⁹ Abram and Nahor took wives; the name of Abram's wife was Sarai, and the name of Nahor's wife was Milcah. She was the daughter of Haran the father of Milcah and Iscah. ³⁰ Now Sarai was barren; she had no child.

Gen 11:31 Terah took his son Abram and his grandson Lot son of Haran, and his daughter-in-law Sarai, his son Abram's wife, and they went out together from Ur of the Chaldeans to go into the land of Canaan; but when they came to Haran, they settled there. ³² The days of Terah were two hundred five years; and Terah died in Haran.

Gen 12:1 Now the Lord said to Abram, 'Go from your country and your kindred and your father's house to the land that I will show you. ² I will make of you a great nation, and I will bless you, and make your name great, so that you will be a blessing. [3] I will bless those who bless you, and the one who curses you I will curse; and in you all the families of the earth shall be blessed.'

Gen 12:4 So Abram went, as the Lord had told him; and Lot went with him. Abram was seventy-five years old when he departed from Haran.

Initial observations

As noted last week, in Lent we have a large story arc from Adam to the Exile; this Sunday introduces the truly foundational figure of Abraham. The excerpt in the lectionary is necessarily brief and the fuller context is given above for ease of understanding.

Kind of writing

Genesis 11:27–30 forms the introduction to the whole Abraham cycle. The telling is highly compressed – 135 years, no less! – so what is selected is important: Sarai is barren. As a result what follows is a totally unexpected new beginning, the call of Abraham.

Genesis 12:1–9 is the beginning of a journey. This is one of the most common plots in traditional heroic literature. What is characteristic of this journey is the initial situation, full of uncertainties. Abraham's goal remains largely in the dark and he will have to discover it little by little.

Origin of the reading

The Book of Genesis divides into four great cycles: Genesis 1–11, the primeval history; Genesis 12–25, the Abraham cycle; Genesis 25–36, the Jacob cycle, and Genesis 37–50, the Joseph cycle (there is no Isaac cycle).

In Rabbinic tradition, the departure of Abraham is the first of *ten* testings of Abraham (the tenth is the sacrifice of Isaac).

The Abraham cycle is prolix (almost prodigal!) in the repeated offering of blessings. Our story is the first of *seven* promises/bestowals of blessing.

Related passages

Outside of Genesis, Abraham is rarely mentioned without the full troika of Abraham, Isaac and Jacob.

> 'Then Joshua gathered all the tribes of Israel to Shechem, and summoned the elders, the heads, the judges, and the officers of Israel; and they presented themselves before God. And Joshua said to all the people, "Thus says the Lord, the God of Israel: Long ago your ancestors — Terah and his sons Abraham and Nahor — lived beyond the Euphrates and served other gods. Then I took your father Abraham from beyond the River and led him through all the land of Canaan and made his offspring many. I gave him Isaac; and to Isaac I gave Jacob and Esau. I gave Esau the hill country of Seir to possess, but Jacob and his children went down to Egypt."' (Joshua 24:1–4)

> 'Wisdom also, when the nations in wicked agreement had been put to confusion, recognised the righteous man and preserved him blameless before God, and kept him strong in the face of his compassion for his child.' (Wisdom 10:5)

Brief commentary

(V. 1)

There is no preparation for this in-breaking of the Lord's voice. Rabbinic tradition notices a threefold command: country, kindred and house. In the tenth testing there is also a threefold, impossibly poignant comment (Genesis 22:2). The link to the sacrifice of Isaac is confirmed in an unusual imperative: *lek leka*, which returns in that later verse: He said, 'Take your son, your only son Isaac, whom you love, and go (*lek leka*) to the land of Moriah' (Genesis 22:2).

(Vv.2–3)

The sevenfold blessing starts here. What does it mean to say 'shall be blessed'? In Hebrew, the verb could be passive (as in the NSRV) or reflexive, 'shall bless themselves'. The reflexive is closer to Jewish piety: may we be as blessed as Abraham was.

(V. 4)

Abraham's obedience is profiled by omitting all personal, psychological and practical consequences.

Seventy-five seems old to us but not in the Bible: Abraham lives until the exceedingly ripe old age of 175. There's a bit to go yet! He has his first child at the age of 100.

Pointers for prayer

a) Inevitably, the reading takes us to our own journey of faith, the call to trust and capacity to set out without knowing the goal. How has that been for me? What events in my life have been affected by it?

b) The leaving of family — a common theme in Genesis — is known to us all. It involves both the pain of parting and the joy of embracing my own journey and identity. Again, how has that been for me in the course of my life?

Prayer

(taken from the *Camino de Santiago*)

O God, who brought your servant Abraham out of the land of the Chaldeans, protecting him in his wanderings, who guided the Hebrew people across the desert, we ask that you watch over us, your servants, as we walk in the love of your name to Santiago de Compostela.

Be for us our companion on the walk, our guide at the crossroads, our breath in our weariness, our protection in danger, our albergue on the Camino, our shade in the heat, our light in the darkness, our consolation in our discouragements, and our strength in our intentions.

So that with your guidance we may arrive safe and sound at the end of the road and, enriched with grace and virtue, we return safely to our homes filled with joy. Through Christ our Lord. Amen.

Themes across the readings

In Jewish and Christian tradition, Abraham is 'our father in faith'. His trust is extraordinary and, in the true sense, radical. No other ancient biblical figure combines in equal measure so many testings and so many blessings.

In Latin (and in Greek), to obey is based on the verb to hear, *ob-audire*. The central teaching of Matthew's version of the Transfiguration is the voice: 'This is my Son, the Beloved; he enjoys my favour. Listen to him.' How to practise this deep listening and obedience from the heart is our challenge. In the language of our time, we would speak of discernment, conversion and discipleship. The opening invitation of *Evangelii Gaudium* expresses it powerfully in relational language.

In some way bridging these two readings, the passage from 2 Timothy invites us, like Abraham, *to rely on the power of God who has saved us and called us to be holy.*

Lent, too, is a pilgrimage of faith, the Christian life in miniature, as we move from conversion (Lent 1) and faith (Lent 2) to the celebration of the great events that give us new life in Christ. In the words of 2 Timothy, *this grace [has] already been granted to us, in Christ Jesus.*

Chapter 3

Lent 3A

Thought for the day

Today we are greatly helped by the wonderful Gospel of the Woman at the Well. On the third attempt, Jesus finally gets through to her, but after that there is no stopping her. As Augustine teaches, she represents us: What do I thirst for? What is the most important thing in my life? Where do I now find God? By relentless challenge and resolute honesty, we too can be led to that encounter with Jesus that changes everything, 'giving life a new horizon and a decisive direction'. May we come to believe because we have heard him ourselves and we know that he really is the saviour of the world.

Prayer

In the midst of the ordinary things, loving God, you call us to the deeper realities: your thirst for us and our thirst for you. Never let us be satisfied, until we come to the springs of living water, welling up for eternal life. Through Christ our Lord. Amen.

 Gospel

Jn 4:5 So he came to a Samaritan city called Sychar, near the plot of ground that Jacob had given to his son Joseph. ⁶ Jacob's well was there, and Jesus, tired out by his journey, was sitting by the well. It was about noon.

Jn 4:7 A Samaritan woman came to draw water, and Jesus said to her, 'Give me a drink.'[8] (His disciples had gone to the city to buy food.) [9] The Samaritan woman said to him, 'How is it that you, a Jew, ask a drink of me, a woman of Samaria?' (Jews do not share things in common with Samaritans.) [10] Jesus answered her, 'If you knew the gift of God, and who it is that is saying to you, "Give me a drink", you would have asked him, and he would have given you living water.' [11] The woman said to him, 'Sir, you have no bucket, and the well is deep. Where do you get that living water?[12] Are you greater than our ancestor Jacob, who gave us the well, and with his sons and his flocks drank from it?' [13] Jesus said to her, 'Everyone who drinks of this water will be thirsty again, [14] but those who drink of the water that I will give them will never be thirsty. The water that I will give will become in them a spring of water gushing up to eternal life.' [15] The woman said to him, 'Sir, give me this water, so that I may never be thirsty or have to keep coming here to draw water.'

Jn 4:16 Jesus said to her, 'Go, call your husband, and come back.' [17] The woman answered him, 'I have no husband.' Jesus said to her, 'You are right in saying, "I have no husband"'; [18] for you have had five husbands, and the one you have now is not your husband. What you have said is true!' [19] The woman said to him, 'Sir, I see that you are a prophet. [20] Our ancestors worshipped on this mountain, but you say that the place where people must worship is in Jerusalem.' [21] Jesus said to her, 'Woman, believe me, the hour is coming when you will worship the Father neither on this mountain nor in Jerusalem. [22] You worship what you do not know; we worship what we know, for salvation is from the Jews. [23] But the hour is coming, and is now here, when the true worshippers will worship the Father in spirit and truth, for the Father seeks such as these to worship him. [24] God is spirit, and those who worship him must worship in spirit and truth.' [25] The woman said to him, 'I know that Messiah is coming' (who is called Christ). 'When he comes, he will proclaim all things to us.' [26] Jesus said to her, 'I am he, the one who is speaking to you.'

Jn 4:27 Just then his disciples came. They were astonished that he was speaking with a woman, but no one said, 'What do you want?' or, 'Why are you speaking with her?' [28] Then the woman left her water jar and went back to the city. She said to the people, [29] 'Come and see a man who told me everything I have ever done! He cannot be the Messiah, can he?' [30] They left the city and were on their way to him.

Jn 4:31 Meanwhile the disciples were urging him, 'Rabbi, eat something.' [32] But he said to them, 'I have food to eat that you do not know about.' [33] So the disciples said to one another, 'Surely no one has brought him something to eat?' [34] Jesus said to them, 'My food is to do the will of him who sent me and to complete his work. [35] Do you not say, "Four months more, then comes the harvest"? But I tell you, look around you, and see how the fields are ripe for harvesting. [36] The reaper is already receiving wages and is gathering fruit for eternal life, so that sower and reaper may rejoice together. [37] For here the saying holds true, "One sows and another reaps." [38] I sent you to reap that for which you did not labour. Others have laboured, and you have entered into their labour.'

Jn 4:39 Many Samaritans from that city believed in him because of the woman's testimony, 'He told me everything I have ever done.' [40] So when the Samaritans came to him, they asked him to stay with them; and he stayed there two days. [41] And many more believed because of his word. [42] They said to the woman, 'It is no longer because of what you said that we believe, for we have heard for ourselves, and we know that this is truly the Saviour of the world.'

Initial observations

This story is found only in the Fourth Gospel. The first four chapters of this Gospel address the different 'constituencies' of the Gospel's readers: followers of the Baptist (1:19–51), the Jews (2:1–12), the Pharisees (3:1–21), the Samaritans (our Gospel today) and the Gentiles (4:46–54). The story is symbolic of the journey of faith, using marriage symbolism from the Old Testament.

Kind of writing

This story is a symbolic narrative, typical of John's Gospel. There may be a remote historical basis, but as it stands it is not historical. Typically for this Gospel (i) there is a one-to-one encounter; (ii) the person encountered makes a considerable journey of faith (Jew, greater than Jacob, prophet, Christ, Saviour of the world); (iii) the exchanges have two layers of meaning (living water = running water). Intriguingly, this woman becomes a herald.

Jesus' question about her husband is only an apparent change of subject – as her next observation shows. Jesus first tries to communicate using the symbolic language of water (= *worship*). He changes his approach, using the (equally) symbolic language of marriage (= *worship*). Finally, he has a breakthrough, using the symbolic language of the temple (= *worship*). Only a later, *moralising* reading thinks of Jesus as exposing the disastrous moral life of the woman, forgetting perhaps that it is not immoral to have five *husbands* — just unlucky.

Old Testament background

(i) Often in the Bible, God's covenant is described as a marriage bond: *You shall no more be termed Forsaken, and your land shall no more be termed Desolate; but you shall be called My Delight Is in Her, and your land Married; for the Lord delights in you, and your land shall be married. For as a young man marries a young woman, so shall your builder marry you, and as the bridegroom rejoices over the bride, so shall your God rejoice over you.* (Isaiah 62:4–5)

OLD TESTAMENT PATTERN	JOHN 4
A man arrives at well	Jesus arrives at Jacob's well
Women come to draw water	The woman comes to draw water
Some 'problem' about the water	Jesus has no bucket; Jews don't share utensils with Samaritans
Recognition scene	Very extended recognition of Jesus
The women go back to tell those at home	The Samaritan woman goes to tell the people in the town
The man is received	Jesus is received.
A wedding!	? But see Jn 4:46!!

(ii) Very often, New Testament stories are based on patterns in the Old Testament, which can be strikingly illuminating. Here, the 'type scene' of meeting your future wife at a well is used, following Jacob (Genesis 29) and Moses (Exodus 2). The pattern is outlined in the box.

(iii) The Samaritans were regarded by their Jewish neighbours as 'mongrel' believers. This helps us to understand the five husbands (= five deities, as we see):

The king of Assyria brought people from *Babylon, Cuthah, Avva, Hamath* and *Sepharvaim*, and placed them in the cities of Samaria in place of the people of Israel; they took possession of Samaria, and settled in its cities. When they first settled there, they did not worship the Lord. (2 Kings 17:24–25a)

New Testament foreground

(i) In John 1–4, bridegroom language is used of Jesus: 2:1–11 and 3:29.

(ii) After the scene at the well, the wedding feast of Cana is invoked, without apparent purpose: 4:46. This recalls the wedding feast and brings in the seventh stage of the type scene — but Jesus is the bridegroom, not of the Samaritans, but of the chosen people, the Jews, and of believing Christians.

(iii) Images combining marriage and water for the Risen Jesus come up again in the Book of Revelation:

> And the angel said to me, 'Write this: Blessed are those who are invited to the marriage supper of the Lamb.' (Revelation 19:9) Then one of the seven angels who had the seven bowls full of the seven last plagues came and said to me, 'Come, I will show you the bride, the wife of the Lamb.' (Revelation 21:9) The Spirit and the bride say, 'Come.' And let everyone who hears say, 'Come.' And let everyone who is thirsty come. Let anyone who wishes take the water of life as a gift. (Revelation 22:17)

St Paul

> I appeal to you therefore, brothers and sisters, by the mercies of God, to present your bodies as a living sacrifice, holy and acceptable to God, which is your spiritual worship. Do not be conformed to this world, but be transformed by the renewing of your minds, so that you may discern what is the will of God – what is good and acceptable and perfect. (Romans 12:1–2)

Brief commentary

(V. 4–6)
The scene is set and our interest awakened. Jacob's well and his marriages (!) are recalled. (The preceding verses 1–3, recalling baptism, are vital to our understanding of this story.) Noon refers to the time Jacob came to the well.

(V. 7–15)
John often uses ironic misunderstandings (clear to the reader) to provoke a deeper insight. 'Living water' and 'running water' are identical in Greek, hence the confusion of the woman. Jesus speaks of a spring ('flowing') while the woman speaks of a well ('stagnant'). The Gospel

reader recalls, of course, John 7:37–39:

> On the last day of the feast, the greatest day, Jesus stood up
> and shouted out, 'If anyone is thirsty, let him come to me, and
> let the one who believes in me drink. Just as the scripture says,
> "From within him will flow rivers of living water". (Now he
> said this about the Spirit, whom those who believed in him
> were going to receive, for the Spirit had not yet been given,
> because Jesus was not yet glorified.) (John 7:37–39 NET
> Bible; the NRSV is not at all accurate here.)

(V. 16–26)
Here we have an apparent change of subject to personal morality —
but actually the subject is that of authentic worship. The woman spots
the change immediately and the conversation continues smoothly about
genuine worship and what God desires of us. The expression 'I am'
echoes Exodus 3:14 and begins the long role of 'I am' sentences unique
to this Gospel (John 4:26; 6:20, 35, 41, 48, 51; 8:12, 18, 24, 28, 58; 9:9;
10:7, 9, 11, 14; 11:25; 13:19; 14:6; 15:1, 5; 18:5–6, 8).

(V. 27–38)
Simultaneous telling is always tricky in narrative. The conversation
with the disciples is a double echo: (i) of the Temptation about bread,
otherwise not in this Gospel and (ii) of the sending out of the Twelve and
the Seventy-two in Matthew, Mark and Luke, also not in this Gospel.
The harvest has begun, including the bringing-in of the Samaritans,
Pharisees, Gentiles and followers of the Baptist.

(V. 39–42)
This completes the sixth stage of the type scene and closes the story with
a very advanced confession of the identity of Jesus. The seventh stage of
the type scene, that is, the wedding, is alluded to in the subsequent verse
46, which recalls the wedding feast of Cana, apparently to no purpose.
Within the tradition, the messiah fulfils God's marriage bond with his
first chosen people, the Jews (represented by the mother in that account).
The final speech of the townspeople is in the symbolic language of the

Johannine community. Compare the wording in 1 John 1:1–4.

> We declare to you what was from the beginning, what we have heard, what we have seen with our eyes, what we have looked at and touched with our hands, concerning the word of life – this life was revealed, and we have seen it and testify to it, and declare to you the eternal life that was with the Father and was revealed to us – we declare to you what we have seen and heard so that you also may have fellowship with us; and truly our fellowship is with the Father and with his Son Jesus Christ. We are writing these things so that our joy may be complete. (1 John 1:1–4)

Pointers for prayer

a) Jesus leads the woman along a wonderful journey towards a deeper and fuller life. You can enter the story with Jesus, the ideal leader, parent, teacher or spiritual guide. Notice how he meets the woman where she is, needing her assistance, how he is patient with her, but also challenges her to grow to what she is capable of. Perhaps you have been such a teacher, or you can recall people who were.

b) You can also enter the story from the perspective of the woman's journey. Notice the steps along the way: suspicion, distrust, curiosity, misunderstanding and conversion. Her journey was one in which a very human motivation attracted her to Jesus: the thought of having water in such a way that she did not have to come and draw it from the well. What have been the human motives that have attracted you to faith, prayer, religion, church, and which have been stepping-stones to a deeper personal relationship with Jesus? Perhaps we can also see the same movement in the growth of some of our human relationships.

c) The woman's final tactic is to attempt to buy time before responding (v. 25) — it will all happen at some time in the future. Jesus points out that the time for a faith response is NOW. How have you discovered the importance of the NOW moment?

Prayer

O God, living and true, look upon your people, whose dry and stony hearts are parched with thirst. Unseal the living water of your Spirit; let it become within us an ever-flowing spring, leaping up to eternal life.

Thus may we worship you in spirit and in truth through Christ, our deliverance and hope, who lives and reigns with you in the unity of the Holy Spirit, holy and mighty God for ever and ever. Amen.

🌿 Second Reading 🌿

Rom 5:1 Therefore, since we have been declared righteous by faith, we have peace with God through our Lord Jesus Christ, ² through whom we have also obtained access by faith into this grace in which we stand, and we rejoice in the hope of God's glory. ³ *Not only this, but we also rejoice in sufferings, knowing that suffering produces endurance,* ⁴ *and endurance, character, and character, hope.* ⁵ And hope does not disappoint, because the love of God has been poured out in our hearts through the Holy Spirit who was given to us.

Rom 5:6 For while we were still helpless, at the right time Christ died for the ungodly. ⁷ (For rarely will anyone die for a righteous person, though for a good person perhaps someone might possibly dare to die.) ⁸ But God demonstrates his own love for us, in that while we were still sinners, Christ died for us.

Initial observations

At first glance, it might seem that the only link between Romans 5 and the other two readings is the word 'poured', taking up the symbolism of water. There is, of course, much more. John's Gospel hints at the gift of the Spirit — picked up in Rom 5:5. At the same time, the reading talks of *access by grace to God*, the very topic of the Woman at the Well.

Kind of writing

The whole of Romans 5–8 parades before the Roman Christians the gifts of grace *in chronological order*, as follows:

Romans 5:	faith, the Spirit, salvation
Romans 6:	baptism
Romans 7:	the moral struggle
Romans 8:	prayer (Abba, Father), the Holy Spirits in our hearts, unshakeable hope in Christ.

Our passage opens the discussion. In an almost imperceptible way, Romans 5:1–5 is an anticipation of all of Romans 5–8, displaying Paul's gift for synthesis. Vv. 6–8 begin the rich discussion of Jesus' death, which will be the main subject of the remaining verses of Romans 5 (see the discussion of vv. 12–19 in last week's notes).

Context in the community

In the Roman house churches, there was conflict between the Christ-believers of Gentile and Christian origin. Paul makes two attempts to break down feelings of separation and superiority. In Romans 1–4, he points out trenchantly that there is no difference between the two groups when it comes to immorality. Both are alike, equally 'successful' in sinning. More constructively in Romans 5–8, he portrays the amazing gifts of grace *shared* by both groups without distinction. Such sheer giftedness, in all its unforeseeable magnificence, undermines – even mocks – any feeling of being superior on our own efforts.

Related passages

> Not only this, but we ourselves also, who have the first-fruits of the Spirit, groan inwardly as we eagerly await our adoption, the redemption of our bodies. For in hope we were saved. Now hope that is seen is not hope, because who hopes for what he sees? But if we hope for what we do not see, we eagerly wait for it with endurance. (Romans 8:23–25)

> And we know that all things work together for good for those who love God, who are called according to his purpose, because those whom he foreknew he also predestined to be conformed to the image of his Son, that his Son would be the firstborn among many brothers and sisters. And those he predestined, he also called; and those he called, he also justified; and those he justified, he also glorified. (Romans 8:28–30)

> All have sinned and fall short of the glory of God. But they are justified freely by his grace through the redemption that is in Christ Jesus. God publicly displayed him at his death as the mercy seat accessible through faith. This was to demonstrate his righteousness, because God in his forbearance had passed over the sins previously committed. This was also to demonstrate his righteousness in the present time, so that he would be just and the justifier of the one who lives because of Jesus' faithfulness. (Romans 3:23–26)

Brief commentary

(V. 1)

Declared righteous means being put into 'right relationship' simply by God's grace. Faith here means two things. It points to the believer's trust, on the model of Abraham in Romans 4. It also points to the faithfulness of Jesus, as explored in Romans 3:21–26. By Jesus' act we have *peace*, that is salvation, with God.

(V. 2)

Key expressions for Paul here are: faith, grace, joy, hope and glory. This is Pauline shorthand for the grand narrative of salvation history, culminating in Christ. In vv. 1–2, salvation is threefold: past, present and future.

(V.3–4)

Paul will take up the topic of our struggle to be faithful in Romans 7, one of the great passages in Paul.

(V. 5)

Here Paul looks forward to the great chapter 8 in Romans, where he will explore both the Holy Spirit and our unshakeable hope in Christ. Even more, for Paul these convictions are an experience of the *love* of God now, 'poured into our hearts'.

(V. 6)

Paul glances back at Romans 1:18–2:29, exploring our incapacity to act in accordance with conscience. He looks forward also to Romans 7: *Wretched man that I am! Who will rescue me from this body of death?* (Romans 7:24) In Paul's teaching on salvation Jesus died for us, meaning *for our benefit* rather than *instead of* (as traditionally understood in atonement theology).

(V. 7)

Even though ancient Greek lacks parentheses, the thought here is parenthetical. It is part of an overall 'all the more so' approach fully exploited in vv. 12–19, as we saw last week.

(V. 8)

NB: Romans 3:21–26 (NET translation). Christ's death discloses God's faithfulness, love and forgiveness, all offered before we even heard of Jesus, not to mention being converted in heart. We are freed from the fundamental human sin of not honouring God precisely as God. Cf. *So the life I now live in the body, I live because of the faithfulness of the Son of God, who loved me and gave himself for me.* (Galatians 2:20)

Pointers for prayer

a) Has the learning in verses 3–4 been my experience?

b) God's breathtaking grace in Christ – when have I recently been aware of the gift, leading to thanksgiving?

Prayer

Always loving God, we stand before you, in awestruck love and gratitude. While were still sinners, you reached out to us in Christ and you still reach out to us today. Help us embrace your love, your forgiveness in Christ, who lives and reigns for ever and ever. Amen.

🍃 First Reading 🍃

Ex 17:1 *From the wilderness of Zin the whole congregation of the Israelites journeyed by stages, as the Lord commanded. They camped at Rephidim, but there was no water for the people to drink.* ² *The people quarrelled with Moses, and said, 'Give us water to drink.' Moses said to them, 'Why do you quarrel with me? Why do you test the LORD?'* ³ But the people thirsted there for water; and the people complained against Moses and said, 'Why did you bring us out of Egypt, to kill us and our children and livestock with thirst?' ⁴ So Moses cried out to the LORD, 'What shall I do with this people? They are almost ready to stone me.' ⁵ The LORD said to Moses, 'Go on ahead of the people, and take some of the elders of Israel with you; take in your hand the staff with which you struck the Nile, and go. ⁶ I will be standing there in front of you on the rock at Horeb. Strike the rock, and water will come out of it, so that the people may drink.' Moses did so, in the sight of the elders of Israel. ⁷ He called the place Massah and Meribah, because the Israelites quarrelled and tested the LORD, saying, 'Is the LORD among us or not?'

Initial observations

This short, perhaps disconcerting, reading is chosen for two reasons. First of all, it continues the story line from Adam to the Exile, with a brief profile of Moses. Secondly, it establishes the imagery of water, which is one of three key metaphors in the Gospel reading.

Apart from such formal considerations, the reading is rich in emotion and feeling. Who has not at times felt that an apparent improvement can feel – at least in the short term – less than satisfactory? There is a second account of this story in the book of Numbers (see below). In that version, this story has a tragic denouement for Moses and Aaron: on account of their apparent disobedience/mistrust, neither will enter the Promised Land. Two opening verses have been included here.

Kind of writing

A brief dramatic incident, available in two traditions. The dominance of water is also a mark of Moses, who was 'saved' by the Nile at birth, took people across the Red Sea and here produced water from the rock.

Origin of the reading

The book of Exodus has the following outline:

The Exodus:	1:1–15:21
Towards Sinai:	15:22–18:27
Sinai covenant:	19:1–24:11
Decalogue/tabernacle:	24:12–31:18
Golden calf incident:	32:1–34:35
Tabernacle:	35:1–40:38

Our passage comes from the journey to Sinai.

Related passages

> Now there was no water for the congregation; so they gathered together against Moses and against Aaron. The

people quarrelled with Moses and said, 'Would that we had died when our kindred died before the Lord! Why have you brought the assembly of the Lord into this wilderness for us and our livestock to die here? Why have you brought us up out of Egypt, to bring us to this wretched place? It is no place for grain, or figs, or vines, or pomegranates; and there is no water to drink.' Then Moses and Aaron went away from the assembly to the entrance of the tent of meeting; they fell on their faces, and the glory of the Lord appeared to them. The Lord spoke to Moses, saying: Take the staff, and assemble the congregation, you and your brother Aaron, and command the rock before their eyes to yield its water. Thus you shall bring water out of the rock for them; thus you shall provide drink for the congregation and their livestock.

So Moses took the staff from before the Lord, as he had commanded him. Moses and Aaron gathered the assembly together before the rock, and he said to them, 'Listen, you rebels, shall we bring water for you out of this rock?' Then Moses lifted up his hand and struck the rock twice with his staff; water came out abundantly, and the congregation and their livestock drank. But the Lord said to Moses and Aaron, 'Because you did not trust in me, to show my holiness before the eyes of the Israelites, therefore you shall not bring this assembly into the land that I have given them.' These are the waters of Meribah, where the people of Israel quarrelled with the Lord, and by which he showed his holiness. (Numbers 20:2–13)

Brief commentary

(V. 1)
Rephidim is the last station before Sinai. (Exodus 19:2; Numbers 33:14–15)

(V. 2)
Testing God means demanding proof that God was really in charge of

what was happening. Cf. v. 7; also: Exodus 8:18; Deuteronomy 7:21; 31:17; Joshua 3:10. The two preceding incidents were also tests. (Exodus 15:25-26 and 16:4)

(V. 3)
Cf. The Israelites said to them, *'If only we had died by the hand of the Lord in the land of Egypt, when we sat by the fleshpots and ate our fill of bread; for you have brought us out into this wilderness to kill this whole assembly with hunger.'* (Exodus 16:3)

(V. 4)
Not the only time!

(V. 5)
The elders function as witnesses here.

(V. 6)
Horeb is the other name for Sinai. Notice that in this J version God commands Moses to strike the rock (contrast the P version in Numbers). The Lord is present, somehow in a visible manner. Cf. *The Lord went in front of them in a pillar of cloud by day, to lead them along the way, and in a pillar of fire by night, to give them light, so that they might travel by day and by night.* (Exodus 13:21)

(V. 7)
Massah = Testing and Meribah = quarrelling. V.7 recalls v.2 above. The names eventually became symbolic of lack of trust, as in Deuteronomy 6:16; 9:22; Ps 95:8.

Pointers for prayer

a) Sometimes after a decision has been made and a new direction taken, we experience regret and doubt. When have I felt this way? Was it a healthy caution or something else?

b) Often as believers, we do wonder where God is in all this mess. This can be general (some incident or other), or quite personal (when a tragedy strikes or things simply turn out very differently). In hindsight, was I able to see God present after all?

Prayer

God, all along the way, you are with us, even when we are not aware or even sure of your presence.

Help us to keep alive our trust in you, 'with us always to the end of the age', so that our life's journey will not be alone or in vain.

We make our prayer through our Lord Jesus Christ, our rock, our spring of living water, who lives and reigns with you and the Holy Spirit, one God, for ever and ever. Amen.

Themes across the readings

The symbolism of water (lightly alluded to in Romans with the phrase 'poured into our hearts') takes us across all three readings. In a very human way, the Old Testament reading voices regret and disappointment with the 'liberation'. A great strength of the reading is that the people at least know that they are thirsty and are able to name their need.

The reading from Romans (why not restore the poetic missing verses 3 and 4?) constitutes a tremendous affirmation of all we have received in Christ. In particular, the Holy Spirit poured into our hearts – the evocation of the Spirit will be fully explored in Romans 8.

John 4 has many levels of meaning. Perhaps three hints may help. It is a story of *pre-evangelisation*, that is the awakening of an unrecognised spiritual thirst. It tells of the *pilgrimage* of faith in Christ, in ever-deepening stages (from being 'a' Jew to the saviour of the world). It illustrates *mission*, as the woman drops her bucket and the real success of mission when the people believe *on their own account*.

Chapter 4

Lent 4A

Thought for the day

How we respond to pressure can vary very much from person to person. In John's Gospel, there are two related stories of people being healed, one in chapter 5 and the other in chapter 9, today's reading. The man at the pool eventually betrays Jesus. The man born blind resists pressure and even grows on the strength of it. Part of his energy comes from his experience – no matter what others may say about Jesus, he himself once was blind and now he sees! His courageous attachment to what he knows from his personal encounter with Jesus leads eventually to a full act of faith.

Prayer

Faithful God, you call us to be faithful even in times of trial. Teach us to embrace the challenge of faith today, that we may have the courage to grow and give courage to others by our witness. Through Christ our Lord. Amen.

🌿 Gospel 🌿

Jn 9:1 As he walked along, he saw a man blind from birth. ² His disciples asked him, 'Rabbi, who sinned, this man or his parents, that he was born blind?' ³ Jesus answered, 'Neither this man nor his parents sinned; he was born blind so that God's works might be revealed in him. ⁴ We must work the works of him who sent me while it is day; night is coming when no one can work. [5] As long as I am in the world, I am the light of the world.' [6] When he had said this, he spat on the ground and made mud with the saliva and spread the mud on the man's eyes, [7] saying to him, 'Go, wash in the pool of Siloam' (which means Sent). Then he went and washed and came back able to see. [8] The neighbours and those who had seen him before as a beggar began to ask, 'Is this not the man who used to sit and beg?' [9] Some were saying, 'It is he.' Others were saying, 'No, but it is someone like him.' He kept saying, 'I am the man.' [10] But they kept asking him, 'Then how were your eyes opened?' [11] He answered, 'The man called Jesus made mud, spread it on my eyes, and said to me, 'Go to Siloam and wash.' Then I went and washed and received my sight.' [12] They said to him, 'Where is he?' He said, 'I do not know.'

Jn 9:13 They brought to the Pharisees the man who had formerly been blind. [14] Now it was a sabbath day when Jesus made the mud and opened his eyes. [15] Then the Pharisees also began to ask him how he had received his sight. He said to them, 'He put mud on my eyes. Then I washed, and now I see.' [16] Some of the Pharisees said, 'This man is not from God, for he does not observe the sabbath.' But others said, 'How can a man who is a sinner perform such signs?' And they were divided. [17] So they said again to the blind man, 'What do you say about him? It was your eyes he opened.' He said, 'He is a prophet.'

Jn 9:18 The Jews did not believe that he had been blind and had received his sight until they called the parents of the man who had received his sight [19] and asked them, 'Is this your son, who you say was born blind? How then does he now see?' [20] His parents answered, 'We know that this is our son, and that he was born blind; [21] but we do not know how it is that now he sees, nor do we know who opened his eyes. Ask him;

he is of age. He will speak for himself.' [22] His parents said this because they were afraid of the Jews; for the Jews had already agreed that anyone who confessed Jesus to be the Messiah would be put out of the synagogue. [23] Therefore his parents said, 'He is of age; ask him.'

Jn 9:24 So for the second time they called the man who had been blind, and they said to him, 'Give glory to God! We know that this man is a sinner.' [25] He answered, 'I do not know whether he is a sinner. One thing I do know, that though I was blind, now I see.' [26] They said to him, 'What did he do to you? How did he open your eyes?' [27] He answered them, 'I have told you already, and you would not listen. Why do you want to hear it again? Do you also want to become his disciples?' [28] Then they reviled him, saying, 'You are his disciple, but we are disciples of Moses. [29] We know that God has spoken to Moses, but as for this man, we do not know where he comes from.' [30] The man answered, 'Here is an astonishing thing! You do not know where he comes from, and yet he opened my eyes. [31] We know that God does not listen to sinners, but he does listen to one who worships him and obeys his will. [32] Never since the world began has it been heard that anyone opened the eyes of a person born blind. [33] If this man were not from God, he could do nothing.' [34] They answered him, 'You were born entirely in sin, and are you trying to teach us?' And they drove him out.

Jn 9:35 Jesus heard that they had driven him out, and when he found him, he said, 'Do you believe in the Son of Man?' [36] He answered, 'And who is he, sir? Tell me, so that I may believe in him.' [37] Jesus said to him, 'You have seen him, and the one speaking with you is he.' [38] He said, 'Lord, I believe.' And he worshipped him. [39] Jesus said, 'I came into this world for judgement so that those who do not see may see, and those who do see may become blind.' [40] Some of the Pharisees near him heard this and said to him, 'Surely we are not blind, are we?' [41] Jesus said to them, 'If you were blind, you would not have sin. But now that you say, "We see", your sin remains.'

Initial observations

This story is found only in the Fourth Gospel, although the other Gospels do tell of blind men (never women!) recovering their sight. Our story, very much longer than in the other Gospels, is the sixth of the seven signs: the Wedding Feast at Cana, Jacob's well, the Royal Official's Son, the Loaves, the Walking on the Water, the Blind Man and Lazarus.

Kind of writing

(i) We have here a short drama, unfolding in a sequence full of suspense:

Scene 1 (1–7a)	A	Jesus and the Blind Man
Scene 2 (7b–12)	B	The Blind Man, neighbours, others
Scene 3 (13–17)	C	The Blind Man, the Pharisees, others
Scene 4 (18–23)	B*	The Blind Man, the Jews, his parents
Scene 5 (24–34)	C*	The Blind Man and the Pharisees
Scene 6 (35–41)	A*	Jesus, the Blind Man, the Pharisees

Dramatically, Jesus is present only in Scenes 1 and 6, but is really present in all the other scenes as well, because his identity is the subject of the investigation. The final scene brings all the chief protagonists together for the first (and last) time. Scene 2 is the confirmation of the cure.

(ii) The 'enquiry' in Scenes 3–5 (structured CBC*) feels both official and threatening, concluding, as it does, with an expulsion. Both these features reflect two issues at the time of writing (about AD 95). The first issue is the obvious one: relations between Jews and 'Christians' had broken down and eventually (perhaps at the 'synod' of Jamnia, c. AD 80) the followers of the Nazarene were expelled from the synagogue (this Gospel alone has the expression 'thrown out of the synagogue' [John 9:22; 12:42; 16:2]). It may well be that family members were under pressure (at the time of writing) when one of them became a Christian. The second issue is that the community of the Beloved Disciple, under a kind of persecution, was obliged to account for its faith ever more clearly and deeply. In hard dialogue with fellow Jews, a profound understanding of the identity of Jesus emerged. We see this in the journey of faith made by the Blind Man: the man, 'I do not know', a prophet, from God, the Son of Man, worshipped him.

Old Testament background

(i) Various aspects of biblical thought should be kept in mind. (a) In the Old Testament, sickness is a result of sin, sometimes parents' sins (e.g. Exodus 20:5); (b) the blind, as handicapped people, may not enter the sanctuary (e.g. Leviticus 21:18); (c) It was forbidden to perform 'works' of any kind on the Sabbath. (d) There is a mild absurdity in the text: when *could* the blind man have *sinned* so that he *would* have been born blind?!?

(ii) The Book of Tobit tells a tale of sight restored and there also it is symbolic.

(iii) Restoration of sight is part of the promise of the Messiah. Compare a text widely alluded to across the New Testament: 'The spirit of the Lord God is upon me, because the Lord has anointed me; he has sent me to bring good news to the oppressed, recovery of sight to the blind [Greek Old Testament addition], to bind up the broken-hearted, to proclaim liberty to the captives, and release to the prisoners' (Isaiah 61:1).

New Testament foreground

(i) Recovery of sight is widely used in the New Testament to speak of coming to faith: e.g. Bartimaeus (Matthew, Mark and Luke) and, most strikingly, Paul himself.

(ii) There are strong links between this story and that of the Woman at the Well (water, pool, the staged journey of faith).

(iii) In this Gospel, Jesus as light frames chapters 1–12 (John 1:4–5, 7–9; 12:35, 46). He has just proclaimed himself Light of the World in John 8:12 and repeats it here in John 9:5.

(iv) 'Seeing', in this Gospel, as often in the New Testament, has two meanings: to see physically and to see (believe) spiritually. The final example in the Gospel is ironic: Blessed are those who have not seen, and yet believe.

(v) The man's journey of faith is facilitated by his lack of certainty:

Jn 9:12 They said to him, 'Where is he?' He said, 'I do not know.' [25] He answered, 'I do not know whether he [= Jesus] is a sinner.' [36] He answered, 'And who is he, sir? Tell me, so that I may believe in him.'

This enabling uncertainty is in contrast to the dead certainties of the man's opponents.

(vi) Jesus finds the man twice, once in: *As he walked along, he saw a man blind from birth* (John 9:1), and then later in: *Jesus heard that they had driven him out, and when he found him, he said, 'Do you believe in the Son of Man?'* (John 9:35)

It is Jesus' recognition of the man's need that leads to a recovery of sight both physical and spiritual. Both are important in the story, because it is the man's first experience of healing, an experience he cannot deny, which opens him to the second healing of faith. He stands by his experience, no matter what the pressure.

St Paul

For it is the God who said, 'Let light shine out of darkness,' who has shone in our hearts to give the light of the knowledge of the glory of God in the face of Jesus Christ. (2 Corinthians 4:6)

Besides this, you know what time it is, how it is now the moment for you to wake from sleep. For salvation is nearer to us now than when we became believers; the night is far gone, the day is near. (Romans 13:11–12)

Brief commentary

(Vv. 1–7a)
This is the symbolic world of light and darkness familiar from John 1:1–18. There is an echo of Genesis 2, where God uses mud to create human beings. Unusually, the man does not seek a cure – Jesus identifies the blindness and offers a cure.

(Vv. 7b–12)
This seeming repetition of the miracle is very important: it establishes that people other than the blind man were aware of the cure. It also establishes the man's personal conviction that something wonderful has happened and no matter what the doctrine it may challenge or contradict, the experience cannot be denied. 'I do not know' is very powerful. Knowing is both positive and negative: the negative knowledge of doctrine, the positive knowledge of experience.

(Vv. 13–17)
The first interview raises a real objection: God cannot both command the Sabbath and be the author of its breaking!? This was a real issue between Jews and the first followers of Jesus.

(Vv. 18–23)
Here a doubt about the authenticity of the cure is raised – hence the parents are interviewed. This may reflect the experience of the community at the time of writing.

(Vv. 24–34)

The grounds of the argument shift to a weaker basis: argument from authority and status. The conflict has had, paradoxically, the opposite effect of making the Blind Man more convinced of his experience and inclined to detach himself from 'the Jews'.

(Vv. 35–41)

All the protagonists are present and a hard judgement is given against those whose certainties are dead.

Pointers for prayer

a) The blind man makes a journey of faith, rooted in an experience of healing from the hand of Jesus. This experience has potential to grow and deepen. What has been my experience of the healing presence of Jesus in my life? Prayer of thanksgiving.

b) Under pressure, the blind man and the community he stands for are obliged to reflect again and again on what they really believe. What has happened to my faith in times of pressure against believing? Prayer of faith.

c) 'Amazing Grace' has the words: *I once was lost, but now I'm found.* Jesus goes out of his way to find the blind man and bring him through the next stage of faith. What has my experience of finding my 'self' been? When have I been touched by Jesus? Is he reaching out to me now? Prayer of conversion.

d) The blind man witnesses to his experience, in spite of conventional, even orthodox opposition. Perhaps this has been part of my experience too? Prayer of witnessing.

When taking a gospel story for prayer, it is often helpful to break the story up into its individual sections. Each section represents a movement, an interaction between the characters. This is particularly true of a long story such as the one we have today. There are six different scenes in this story. Any one of them could be the focal point for your prayer. Try to identify the movement in the section you take for prayer. The objective is to discover the Good News in the story. The Good News is that the story of grace is deeper than the story of sin, both in the Gospels and in our lives. One should also note the different characters in the story, for each of them could be a character with whom you can identify. In this story we have Jesus, the blind beggar, the disciples, the neighbours, the blind man's parents and the Pharisees.

Prayer

God, our Creator, show forth your mighty works in the midst of your people. Enlighten your Church, that we may know your Son as the true light of the World and through our worship confess him as Christ and Lord, who lives and reigns with you in the unity of the Holy Spirit, holy and mighty God for ever and ever. Amen.

🌿 Second Reading 🌿

Eph 5:7 *Therefore do not be associated with them.* [8] For once you were darkness, but now in the Lord you are light. Live as children of light – [9] for the fruit of the light is found in all that is good and right and true. [10] Try to find out what is pleasing to the Lord. [11] Take no part in the unfruitful works of darkness, but instead expose them. [12] For it is shameful even to mention what such people do secretly; [13] but everything exposed by the light becomes visible, [14] for everything that becomes visible is light. Therefore it says,

Sleeper, awake!
Rise from the dead,
and Christ will shine on you.

Initial observations

The imagery of light makes this reading especially inviting and appropriate for the fourth Sunday of Lent. It functions as a kind of encouragement not to lose heart but to keep on going in view of the great hope we have in the risen Christ, to be celebrated soon at Easter.

Kind of writing

Ephesians has a simple letter layout:

1:1–2	Greeting
1:3–14	Blessing
1:15–23	Thanksgiving
2:1–6:20	*Body of the Letter*
7:21–24	Letter conclusion

Overall, Ephesians reflects a common type of writing at the time, the Two Ways form of instruction. Our reading comes from a portion of the body of the letter devoted to living as children of the light (Ephesians 5:1–14).

It is really unlikely that the letter is from Paul. The practice of writing in the name of another was well known at the time. It allowed one to acknowledge the main source of one's ideas, while bringing the tradition up to date in a new context.

Context in the community

Ephesians is a document of second generation Paulinism. Like Colossians in many ways (perhaps a second, expanded edition?), it nonetheless has its own deeper teaching about Christ, as we can see in Ephesians 5:21–6:2. The context is a later one and the challenge is how to sustain the message of Paul and bring it to expression for a later generation. Not really unlike our own time, when you think about it.

Related passages

> Now this I affirm and insist on in the Lord: you must no
> longer live as the Gentiles live, in the futility of their minds.
> They are darkened in their understanding, alienated from the
> life of God because of their ignorance and hardness of heart.
> They have lost all sensitivity and have abandoned themselves
> to licentiousness, greedy to practise every kind of impurity.
> (Ephesians 4:17–19)

> For our struggle is not against enemies of blood and flesh, but
> against the rulers, against the authorities, against the cosmic
> powers of this present darkness, against the spiritual forces of
> evil in the heavenly places. (Ephesians 6:12)

> But you, beloved, are not in darkness, for that day to surprise
> you like a thief; for you are all children of light and children
> of the day; we are not of the night or of darkness. So then let
> us not fall asleep as others do, but let us keep awake and be
> sober. (1 Thessalonians 5:4–6)

Brief commentary

(V. 7)

Following on a list of vices in vv. 3-6, v. 7 looks on and looks forward,
opening up the positive reflection of living in the light. The teaching is
not unlike that found in 2 Corinthians 6:14–7:1.

(V. 8)

The train of thought is quite Pauline – the *indicative* of what you are
followed by the *imperative* of what you should become. As in the Dead
Sea Scrolls, use is made of a moderate dualism to delineate conduct
sharply.

(V. 9)

Using a slightly mixed metaphor, the author encourages good behaviour.
There is a discussion about the intended audience at this point — pagans
or believers. On balance, it is more likely the advice is to Christ-believers.

(V. 10)

The verb used could also be translated as to *discern* what is pleasing to the Lord. In the cultural context, determining what is suitable behaviour is an activity of reason. For the believer, in contrast, the 'locus' of such discernment is our relationship with the risen Christ.

(V. 11)

The 'unfruitful works of darkness' is a general reference to the ways of unbelievers. Who is addressed here? It might be fellow believers who have slipped back into former practices (Matthew 18:15–17; Galatians 6:1). Or, are we to think of believers, at this point, rebuking outsiders for their behaviour? This latter is preferable in light of vv. 12–13. The Church must not retreat from the world but confront it.

(Vv. 12–13)

Given the list of vices early in chapter 5, it is likely that the writer has in mind sexual immorality and indecency. It may even be that Christians – by standing apart from society – are already being accused of some kind of secret activity. The affirmations here are rather general, but, perhaps were clearer to the first hearers than to later readers. There is an echo of the teaching of Jesus: *For there is nothing hidden, except to be disclosed; nor is anything secret, except to come to light.* (Mark 4:22)

(V. 14)

The three lines in poetic form are most likely an excerpt from a baptismal hymn, presumably familiar to the audience. The references are to baptism and to the Lord's Day, marking the resurrection. Cf. *Arise, shine; for your light has come, and the glory of the Lord has risen upon you.* (Isaiah 60:1)

Pointers for prayer

a) As we approach Easter, this is a good time to reflect on being baptised – how have I appropriated the gift as a grown-up?

b) Challenging the surrounding culture is, well, challenging. What has my experience been? What have I learned?

Prayer

Father of light, you have called us into being and called us again to new life in Christ. As we received the light of Christ in faith and baptism, help us to be what we have received and to live as children of the light. Through Christ our Lord. Amen.

🌿 First Reading 🌿

1 Sam 16:1 The LORD said to Samuel, 'How long will you grieve over Saul? I have rejected him from being king over Israel. Fill your horn with oil and set out; I will send you to Jesse the Bethlehemite, for I have provided for myself a king among his sons.'² Samuel said, 'How can I go? If Saul hears of it, he will kill me.' And the LORD said, 'Take a heifer with you, and say, 'I have come to sacrifice to the LORD.'³ Invite Jesse to the sacrifice, and I will show you what you shall do; and you shall anoint for me the one whom I name to you.'⁴ Samuel did what the Lord commanded, and came to Bethlehem. The elders of the city came to meet him trembling, and said, 'Do you come peaceably?'⁵ He said, 'Peaceably; I have come to sacrifice to the Lord; sanctify yourselves and come with me to the sacrifice.' And he sanctified Jesse and his sons and invited them to the sacrifice.

1 Sam 16:6 When they came, he looked on Eliab and thought, 'Surely the Lord's anointed is now before the LORD.'⁷ But the Lord said to Samuel, 'Do not look on his appearance or on the height of his stature, because I have rejected him; for the LORD does not see as mortals see; they look on the outward appearance, but the LORD looks on the heart.'⁸ Then Jesse called Abinadab, and made him pass before Samuel. He said, 'Neither has the Lord chosen this one.'⁹ Then Jesse made

Shammah pass by. And he said, 'Neither has the LORD chosen this one.' [10] Jesse made seven of his sons pass before Samuel, and Samuel said to Jesse, 'The LORD has not chosen any of these.' [11] Samuel said to Jesse, 'Are all your sons here?' And he said, 'There remains yet the youngest, but he is keeping the sheep.' And Samuel said to Jesse, 'Send and bring him; for we will not sit down until he comes here.' [12] He sent and brought him in. Now he was ruddy, and had beautiful eyes, and was handsome. The LORD said, 'Rise and anoint him; for this is the one.' [13] Then Samuel took the horn of oil, and anointed him in the presence of his brothers; and the spirit of the Lord came mightily upon David from that day forward. Samuel then set out and went to Ramah.

Initial observations

Our reading takes us to another great character in the biblical tradition: David. Many scenes could have been chosen but this is selected on account of the emphasis on the seeing of God.

Kind of writing

This delightful vignette is a quest story.

Exposition:	1–4a Context and actors
Complication:	4b–11 Suspense
Climax:	12 David identified
Denouement:	13 Anointing as king

Style: A key word guides the narrative: the verb to see (1 Samuel 16:1, 6–7). It is not always clear in translation.

Tension: The prophet's first discernment is mistaken and God has to intervene directly (v. 7). The parade of sons creates tension, even though we are spared the tedium of plodding repetition with the use of the *et cetera* principle (v. 10).

Reading stance: the first-time hearer/reader will be on the same level of information as the characters in the story. At that level of even-handed telling, the focus will be on the person selected.

Finally: It is rare in the Bible for a character to be described physically. For the regular Bible reader v. 12a is unusual.

David is also the youngest, an echo of a powerful theme in Genesis known as the reversal of primogeniture.

Origin of the reading

The books of Samuel constitute a meditation on kingship in Israel. Apart from the monarchs, Samuel is the most important character. Within the two books of Samuel, the prophet himself is a complex and ambiguous figure. To catch a sense of that, it would be good to read 1 Samuel 8.

Related passages

> Jesse became the father of Eliab his firstborn, Abinadab the second, Shimea the third, Nethanel the fourth, Raddai the fifth, Ozem the sixth, David the *seventh*. (1 Chronicles 2:13–15)

Brief commentary

(V. 1)
The grieving links this story with the previous one in 1 Samuel 15. Saul was indeed eventually rejected: see 1 Samuel 15:23 as well as 8:7; 10:19; 15:26.

(V. 2a)
Samuel fears Saul's reaction to his subversion.

(Vv. 2b–3)
God proposes a subterfuge to gain entry to Jesse's family so that the next monarch may be discerned.

(Vv. 4–5)

The arrival of Samuel causes alarm, which the prophet deals with. In this way, access is gained.

(Vv. 6–7)

Suspense begins with the prophet's false discernment, quickly set aside by God. Looking at appearances was the mistake before because Saul was also tall (1 Samuel 9:22; 10:23). V. 7b is a key to the point of the whole story.

(Vv. 8–10)

The parade is quickly told and even abbreviated. It seems the story at this point is blocked: *none* of the sons of Jesse is suitable.

(V. 11)

To be sure, Samuel asks a question. David is identified as the youngest and as a shepherd. Kings were often compared to pastors in the ancient Near East. David's youth is a reference to the elevation of the youngest in Genesis, itself a symbol of God's selection of insignificant Israel as his chosen people. The postponement of hospitality creates a final tension, quickly told.

(V. 12)

The unusual description gives David great 'presence' in the telling because the reader/hearer is invited to imagine him. We notice in v. 12b that it is not Samuel who speaks but the Lord himself. Samuel was in error before – just now with the sons of Jesse and, more alarmingly, with Saul as king.

(V. 13)

The traditional anointing takes place in the restricted circle of the family to keep it secret. The spirit of the Lord is given here for the grace of leadership. See 1 Samuel 10:6; 16:13–14; 2 Samuel 23:2; 1 Kings 18:12; 22:24; 2 Kings 2:16.

Pointers for prayer

a) We all tend to look at appearances. What has helped me in my life to look deeper?

b) Sometimes the unexpected choice really is the right one. Can I see that in my own life experience?

Prayer

You yourself, O God, are our light and you have 'shone in our hearts to give the light of the knowledge of the glory of God in the face of Jesus Christ'. Help us to receive this gift with faith and become people who live not by appearances but by the inner light of truth and faith.
Through Christ our Lord. Amen.

Themes across the readings

Our first reading portrays a prophet who cannot see very well, because he sees as humans do. In a way, God has to step in to (over)see the election. The key phrase is: *but the Lord looks on the heart* (1 Samuel 16:7). The theme of God's guidance in darkness continues in the psalm.

The excerpt from Ephesians profiles light in contrast to darkness. Key words: light, illuminate, shine, used of coming to faith in Christ, lead us to the brilliant story of the man born blind.

The Gospel story – also a quest – serves to explore one of the 'I am' sentences of the Fourth Gospel: *Again Jesus spoke to them, saying, 'I am the light of the world. Whoever follows me will never walk in darkness but will have the light of life.'* (John 8:12) *'As long as I am in the world, I am the light of the world.'* (John 9:5) The seeing of faith is bestowed by the one who is our light.

Chapter 5

Lent 5 A

Thought for the day

The historical Jesus was guarded in declaring his identity, but by the time the Fourth Gospel was written, Christians had arrived at a rich understanding of the mystery of Jesus, the Son of God. John's Gospel puts before the believer a grand assemblage of seven I AM sentences, rooted in the name of God in Exodus 3:14, I AM WHO I AM. *I am the bread of life.* (John 6:35, 48, 51); *I am the light of the world* (John 8:12; 9:5); *I am the gate for the sheep* (John 10:7, 9); *I am the good shepherd* (John 10:11, 14); *I am the resurrection and the life* (John 11:25); *I am the way, and the truth, and the life* (John 14:6); *I am the true vine* (John 15:1, 5). We are reminded that we believe first of all in a person, not in a philosophy. Any one of these images would take us deeply into our encounter with the Risen Lord, none more so than '*I am the resurrection and the life.*'

Prayer

Jesus, present to us always, you wept at the tomb of your friend Lazarus. As we face the mystery of death, our own and that of those we love, help us to place our trust in you, the resurrection and the life, for ever and ever. Amen.

 Gospel

Jn 11:1 Now a certain man was ill, Lazarus of Bethany, the village of Mary and her sister Martha. ² Mary was the one who anointed the Lord with perfume and wiped his feet with her hair; her brother Lazarus was ill. ³ So the sisters sent a message to Jesus, 'Lord, he whom you love is ill.'⁴ But when Jesus heard it, he said, 'This illness does not lead to death; rather it is for God's glory, so that the Son of God may be glorified through it.'⁵ Accordingly, though Jesus loved Martha and her sister and Lazarus, ⁶ after having heard that Lazarus was ill, he stayed two days longer in the place where he was.

Jn 11:7 Then after this he said to the disciples, 'Let us go to Judea again.'⁸ The disciples said to him, 'Rabbi, the Jews were just now trying to stone you, and are you going there again?'⁹ Jesus answered, 'Are there not twelve hours of daylight? Those who walk during the day do not stumble, because they see the light of this world. ¹⁰ But those who walk at night stumble, because the light is not in them.'¹¹ After saying this, he told them, 'Our friend Lazarus has fallen asleep, but I am going there to awaken him.' ¹² The disciples said to him, 'Lord, if he has fallen asleep, he will be all right.' ¹³ Jesus, however, had been speaking about his death, but they thought that he was referring merely to sleep. ¹⁴ Then Jesus told them plainly, 'Lazarus is dead. ¹⁵ For your sake I am glad I was not there, so that you may believe. But let us go to him.'¹⁶ Thomas, who was called the Twin, said to his fellow disciples, 'Let us also go, that we may die with him.'

Jn 11:17 When Jesus arrived, he found that Lazarus had already been in the tomb four days. ¹⁸ Now Bethany was near Jerusalem, some two miles away, ¹⁹ and many of the Jews had come to Martha and Mary to console them about their brother. ²⁰ When Martha heard that Jesus was coming, she went and met him, while Mary stayed at home. ²¹ Martha said to Jesus, 'Lord, if you had been here, my brother would not have died. ²² But even now I know that God will give you whatever you ask of him.' ²³ Jesus said to her, 'Your brother will rise again.' ²⁴ Martha said to him, 'I know that he will rise again in the resurrection on the last day.' ²⁵ Jesus said to her, 'I am the resurrection and the life. Those who believe in me, even though they die, will live, ²⁶ and everyone who lives and believes in me will never die. Do you believe this?' ²⁷ She said to him, 'Yes, Lord, I believe that you are the Messiah, the Son of God, the one coming into the world.'

Jn 11:28 When she had said this, she went back and called her sister Mary, and told her privately, 'The Teacher is here and is calling for you.' ²⁹ And when she heard it, she got up quickly and went to him. ³⁰ Now Jesus had not yet come to the village, but was still at the place where Martha had met him. ³¹ The Jews who were with her in the house, consoling her, saw Mary get up quickly and go out. They followed her because they thought that she was going to the tomb to weep there. ³² When Mary came where Jesus was and saw him, she knelt at his feet and said to him, 'Lord, if you had been here, my brother would not have died.' ³³ When Jesus saw her weeping, and the Jews who came with her also weeping, he was greatly disturbed in spirit and deeply moved. ³⁴ He said, 'Where have you laid him?' They said to him, 'Lord, come and see.' ³⁵ Jesus began to weep. ³⁶ So the Jews said, 'See how he loved him!' ³⁷ But some of them said, 'Could not he who opened the eyes of the blind man have kept this man from dying?'

Jn 11:38 Then Jesus, again greatly disturbed, came to the tomb. It was a cave, and a stone was lying against it. ³⁹ Jesus said, 'Take away the stone.' Martha, the sister of the dead man, said to him, 'Lord, already there is a stench because he has been dead four days.' ⁴⁰ Jesus said to her, 'Did I not tell you that if you believed, you would see the glory of God?' ⁴¹ So they took away the stone. And Jesus looked upward and said, 'Father, I thank you for having heard me. ⁴² I knew that you always hear me, but I have said this for the sake of the crowd standing here, so that they may believe that you sent me.' ⁴³ When he had said this, he cried with a loud voice, 'Lazarus, come out!' ⁴⁴ The dead man came out, his hands and feet bound with strips of cloth, and his face wrapped in a cloth. Jesus said to them, 'Unbind him, and let him go.'

Jn 11:45 Many of the Jews therefore, who had come with Mary and had seen what Jesus did, believed in him.

Initial observations

This story is found only in the Fourth Gospel, although the other Gospels do tell of people being raised from the dead (Jairus's daughter, the son of the widow of Nain). Our story, very much longer than these other stories, is the seventh (the climax) of the seven signs: the Wedding Feast at Cana, the Woman at the Well, the Royal Official's Son, the Loaves, the Walking on the Water, the Blind Man and the Raising of Lazarus. The writer has expanded the narrative into a moving drama, thus exploring in a very human way the teaching about Jesus and the resurrection.

Kind of writing

This is the last and most significant symbolic tableau in the Fourth Gospel. It explores the meaning of the resurrection of Jesus for believers. It is the climax of 'seven signs', which undergird the narrative of the Fourth Gospel, thus taking us to the heart of this Gospel's teaching.

Old Testament background

(i) By and large in the Old Testament, there is no real conviction about a genuine life after death. There *are* exceptions. Ezekiel, writing during the Babylonian Exile (587–39 BC) and, speaking metaphorically, describes the future restoration of the next generation using the language of resurrection (Ezekiel 37 – the Valley of the Dry Bones). The Book of Daniel teaches the resurrection (Daniel 12:2), as does 2 Maccabees 12. The context there is martyrdom. In that context, the question of God's faithfulness to those who have been faithful till death became acute. In order to continue to speak of God as just, a teaching about reward and resurrection in the next life emerged. The driving force is not speculation about the human condition but the need to continue to speak of God as just. Finally, in some of the psalms there is a possible hint at something more: Psalms 16:9–11, 49:15.

(ii) The Fourth Gospel has many 'I am' sentences on the lips of Jesus: I am the bread of life, the true vine, the Good Shepherd, the light of the world, the way, the truth and life. These are intentional echoes of God's self-revelation to Moses as I AM WHO I AM (Exodus 3:14).

New Testament foreground

(i) *Links with the rest of the Gospel* (relatively unusual in this text):

Lazarus is mentioned elsewhere: 12:1, 9, 17. *Mary* appears again in 12:3. She is not Mary Magdalene. *Martha* gets mentioned in 12:2. *Caiaphas* returns in 18:13, 14, 24, 28. *Thomas* 14:5; 20:24, 26; 21:2. *Judas* (6:71); 12:4; 13:2, 26, 29; 14:22; 18:2, 3, 5. *Pharisees* 12:19, 42; 18:3.

There is also an unusual direct reference to a previous story – the man born blind – the link is Jesus himself, as the one having light and giving sight.

(ii) *Location within the Gospel:*

The full setting is over two and a half chapters, John 10:40–12:11, unfolded over five grand scenes, resembling a play or a drama.

I   Across the Jordan (= Bethany), many believed in him (10:40–42)
II   Jesus, Lazarus, Mary, Martha, Bethany; cross-references (11:2) and burial (11:1–44)
III This is the centre – because the plot against Jesus takes off (11:45–57)

II* Jesus, Lazarus, Mary, Martha, Bethany; cross-references (11:2) and burial (12:1–8)

I* House of Lazarus (= Bethany); many believed in him (12:9–11). Within that wider 'plot', our story has its own outline and centre.

(iii) *Our Gospel excerpt:*

Our excerpt, 11:1–45, is no. **II** above, with a line from **III.** It exhibits its own meaningful pattern, where the physical central passage (**C.** in the chart) is also the centre of meaning.

A. vv. 1–19 Jesus, the illness and death Lazarus, the disciples and the Jews
  B. vv. 20–22 Jesus and Martha
    C. vv. 23–27 Jesus reveals himself as the resurrection and the life
  B* vv. 28–32 Jesus and Mary
A* vv. 33–44 Jesus, the resurrection of Lazarus, Mary and Martha, and the Jews

> Jesus said to her, 'Your brother will rise again.' Martha said to him, 'I know that he will rise again in the resurrection on the last day.' Jesus said to her, 'I am the resurrection and the life. Those who believe in me, even though they die, will live, and everyone who lives and believes in me will never die. Do you believe this?' She said to him, 'Yes, Lord, I believe that you are the Messiah, the Son of God, the one coming into the world.' (John 11:23–27)

(iv) Jesus preached the Kingdom of God; the earliest communities preached the king, Jesus risen from the dead. The Johannine community takes this one step deeper and teaches not only that Jesus is risen, but that he is himself personally the Resurrection. Our trust is not in a teaching but in a person. This conviction emerges earlier in the Gospel and, in many ways, today's Gospel excerpt is a comment on this momentous earlier passage:

> Indeed, just as the Father raises the dead and gives them life, so also the Son gives life to whomever he wishes. The Father judges no one but has given all judgement to the Son, so that

all may honour the Son just as they honour the Father. Anyone who does not honour the Son does not honour the Father who sent him. Very truly, I tell you, anyone who hears my word and believes him who sent me has eternal life, and does not come under judgement, but has passed from death to life. 'Very truly, I tell you, the hour is coming, and is now here, when the dead will hear the voice of the Son of God, and those who hear will live. For just as the Father has life in himself, so he has granted the Son also to have life in himself; and he has given him authority to execute judgement, because he is the Son of Man. Do not be astonished at this; for the hour is coming when all who are in their graves will hear his voice and will come out – those who have done good, to the resurrection of life, and those who have done evil, to the resurrection of condemnation. 'I can do nothing on my own. As I hear, I judge; and my judgement is just, because I seek to do not my own will but the will of him who sent me. (John 5:21–30)

(v) There are important links with the resurrection of Jesus himself:

> The dead man came out, his hands and feet bound with strips of cloth, and his face wrapped in a cloth. Jesus said to them, 'Unbind him, and let him go.' (John 11:44)

> Then Simon Peter came, following him, and went into the tomb. He saw the linen wrappings lying there, and the cloth that had been on Jesus' head, not lying with the linen wrappings but rolled up in a place by itself. (John 20:6–7)

The unusual detail about the headband serves two purposes, to connect and distinguish the resurrection of Jesus and that of Lazarus. The distinction: the resurrection of Lazarus is qualitatively different – he still needs to be unbound; contrariwise, the resurrection of Jesus is definitive and effective – he no longer needs unbinding, but has passed from death to life. The connection: Jesus raised Lazarus because he loved him (11:36: 'See how much he loved him').

The Fourth Gospel teaches that, just as Jesus dies for love of us (3:16a), he also rises from the dead for love of us (3:16b). In a word, the gift of new life transcending death is the measure of the love of God for humanity and for each of us. This aspect of resurrection faith is brought out uniquely in this Gospel, especially by the careful linking of the raising of Lazarus and the rising of Jesus.

St Paul

It is the same with the resurrection of the dead. What is sown is perishable, what is raised is imperishable. It is sown in dishonour, it is raised in glory; it is sown in weakness, it is raised in power; it is sown a natural body, it is raised a spiritual body. If there is a natural body, there is also a spiritual body. So also it is written, 'The first man, Adam, became a living person'; the last Adam became a life-giving spirit. However, the spiritual did not come first, but the natural, and then the spiritual. The first man is from the earth, made of dust; the second man is from heaven. Like the one made of dust, so too are those made of dust, and like the one from heaven, so too those who are heavenly. And just as we have borne the image of the man of dust, let us also bear the image of the man of heaven. (1 Corinthians 15:42–49)

Brief commentary

(Vv. 1–5)
The narrative opens with the significant people named and the problem – Lazarus' illness and death – is identified. V. 2 is an anticipation of chapter 12. V. 4 alerts the reader to a different level of meaning.

(V. 6)
This is a surprise (creating suspense), especially after the story of the Blind Man, where Jesus initiates the cure. The delay – unexpected and unexplained – seems not to make sense.

(Vv. 7–10)
The disciples try to dissuade Jesus from making a journey that could threaten his life, unaware that the cross leads to resurrection. V. 9 recalls 'I AM the light of the world' from chapters 8 and 9.

(Vv. 11–16)

As often in this Gospel, people close to Jesus radically misunderstand him. The reader is invited to reflect deeply, looking at these stories with the 20:20 vision of Easter hindsight.

Vv. 17–27

Jesus and Martha: a disclosure leads to an act of faith. This is an intense one-to-one encounter, typical of this Gospel and resembling the previous quest stories of the Samaritan woman and the man born blind

(Vv. 28–32)

Jesus and Mary: the gesture of imploring implies faith. This is a second, even more intense one-to-one encounter.

(Vv. 33–43)

Jesus himself is moved profoundly to act for his friend. Certainly, this is the emotional and theological climax of our Gospel excerpt.

(V. 44)

The 'illness' of Lazarus is reversed; note, however, that he has to be nevertheless unbound – unlike Jesus in this Gospel: … *the cloth that had been on Jesus' head, not lying with the linen wrappings but rolled up in a place by itself.* (John 20:7)

(V. 45)

This apparent affirmation leads directly to the plot against Jesus, as the very next verse (46) makes clear.

This intensely human account has a profoundly consoling message: the resurrection, realised and offered in the person of Jesus, is the supreme gesture of God's love towards humanity. In Jesus, God reaches out to the tragedy of the human condition and to each one of us. This is the 'tender mercy' of our God. (Luke 1:78)

Pointers for prayer

a) Martha and Mary are portrayed as people of faith but Jesus led them to an even deeper faith. Who were the people who led you to a deeper faith in Jesus? Remember them and give thanks.

b) Martha and Mary were struggling to come to terms with their bereavement. What has helped you in similar situations?

c) The concern of Jesus is palpable and touching. Recall those who matter to you and to whom you matter. Such love mediates God's love, which surpasses human love with the gift of new life and Easter joy.

d) One can imagine Lazarus as a symbol of people and groups that are written off as dead (sometimes by themselves), and yet through faith come back to life again. Have you had the experience of being revived by faith? Has faith helped to free you from what held you in bondage or was destructive of your life?

Prayer

Merciful God, you showed your glory to our fallen race by sending your Son to confound the powers of death.

Call us forth from sin's dark tomb: break the bonds which hold us, that we may believe and proclaim Christ the cause of our freedom and the source of life, who lives and reigns with you in the unity of the Holy Spirit, holy and mighty God, for ever and ever. Amen.

🌿 Second Reading 🌿

Rom 8:8 Those who are in the flesh cannot please God. ⁹ You, however, are not in the flesh but in the Spirit, if indeed the Spirit of God lives in you. Now if anyone does not have the Spirit of Christ, this person does not belong to him. ¹⁰ But if Christ is in you, your body is dead because of sin, but the Spirit is your life because of righteousness. ¹¹ Moreover if the

Spirit of the one who raised Jesus from the dead lives in you, the one who raised Christ from the dead will also make your mortal bodies alive through his Spirit who lives in you.

Initial observations

The readings for the fourth Sunday of Lent are exceptionally united around the resurrection. Our passage from Romans brings its own perspective, which focuses not only on our *future* afterlife but also on our *present* life in the Spirit. This gives the second reading an immediate and practical relevance.

Kind of writing

Paul's account of all we have received in Christ comes to a climax with this great 'hymn' to the Holy Spirit.

Context in the community

Within the Roman Christian house churches, a conflict had arisen over how much of the Torah regulations to retain. It looks as if Christian believers of Gentile background did not observe the dietary laws etc., and, in their 'higher' freedom, looked down on those who did keep such laws. On the other hand, Christian believers of Jewish origin put a great deal of store on their fidelity to tradition and, in their 'greater' faithfulness, looked down on those who did not keep the Law. In the first four chapters of Romans, Paul destabilises both groups, showing that they are equally 'successful' in sinning and equally in need of both grace and faith. Moving from this negative evaluation, in chapters 5–8, Paul lays out in chronological order the wonderful gifts of salvation received by all. His purpose is once more to show that, both at the level of need and at the level of grace, 'there is no distinction' because 'God has no favourites.'

Related passages

The role of the Holy Spirit is evident from the very start of Romans:

> Therefore, since we have been declared righteous by faith, we have peace with God through our Lord Jesus Christ, through whom we have also obtained access by faith into this grace in which we stand, and we rejoice in the hope of God's glory. Not only this, but we also rejoice in sufferings, knowing that suffering produces endurance, and endurance, character, and character, hope. And hope does not disappoint, because *the love of God has been poured out in our hearts through the Holy Spirit who was given to us.* (Romans 5:1–5)

Romans 8 should be read as a whole to see the role and significance of the Spirit in St Paul's theology: Rom 8:2, 4–6, 9–11, 13–16, 23, 26–27. See also 1 Corinthians and Galatians:

> God has revealed these to us by the Spirit. For the Spirit searches all things, even the deep things of God. For who among men knows the things of a man except the man's spirit within him? So, too, no one knows the things of God except the Spirit of God. Now we have not received the spirit of the world, *but the Spirit who is from God, so that we may know the things that are freely given to us by God.* (1 Corinthians 2:10–12)

> Now the works of the flesh are obvious: sexual immorality, impurity, depravity, idolatry, sorcery, hostilities, strife, jealousy, outbursts of anger, selfish rivalries, dissensions, factions, envying, murder, drunkenness, carousing, and similar things. I am warning you, as I had warned you before: Those who practise such things will not inherit the kingdom of God! *But the fruit of the Spirit is love, joy, peace, patience, kindness, goodness, faithfulness, gentleness and self-control.* Against such things there is no law. (Galatians 5:19–23)

Brief commentary

(V. 8)

While it can be confusing, it is evident that flesh does not refer to the body or to material existence. Later, in Christian spirituality under the influence of Platonism, a distinction did indeed arise between the high spiritual self and the lower bodily self. But Paul remains Jewish and respects the biblical intuition that the material order is God's creation and therefore good in itself. By 'flesh', Paul means our whole human nature as such, viewed as belonging to this world, that is, apart from God and Christ, being both independent and powerless.

(V. 9)

The affirmation in v. 9 makes it clear that flesh is not the body as such, because the Romans are definitely 'in the body'! To be in the Spirit means to have received the Spirit and to have the mind of Christ. The verse is in two parts, saying the same thing first positively and then negatively. The indwelling of the Spirit echoes God's presence or *shekinah* in the Temple, now realised in the hearts of all believers. (For Paul, Spirit, Spirit of God and Spirit of Christ are all the one presence and gift.)

(V. 10)

Christ himself is in believers' hearts because of the Spirit's indwelling. The body being dead is a reference to the human condition under the power of sin and death, explored earlier in Romans 5 in the discussion of Adam. Physical/bodily death is the evidence and proof of this condition. By contrast, the Holy Spirit counteracts the power of sin and death by making alive in our hearts the righteousness of God – God's faithfulness and compassion disclosed in Jesus and given to us in the Spirit (Romans 3:21–26). As a result, we too can be both faithful and righteous, *in this present life*.

(V. 11)

This verse is the climax of this reflection. God's faithfulness to Jesus in resurrection is the first instalment of God's faithfulness to all humanity.

Jesus' resurrection – the first fruits of all who sleep – already anticipates and enables our own resurrection. The indwelling Spirit, a kind of down payment (2 Corinthians 1:22), is the guarantee, even proof, of that future reality. Our bodily reality, far from being neglected or set aside, will also be part of that new reality, however we may imagine it (see 1 Corinthians 15:35–49).

Pointers for prayer

a) Living 'without God' is part of all our experience, at least from time to time. Can I recognise this reality in myself?

b) God's presence within – his *shekinah* in all of us through Jesus' Spirit – means that our prayer is simply a 'yes' to gift and reality.

Prayer

O God, you are within us all, through the Holy Spirt. Help us to acknowledge your gift and presence through prayer and meditation. Help us to live the gift of your faithfulness by being faithful to you in how we live and move and have our being. Through Christ our Lord. Amen.

First Reading

Ezek 37:11 *Then he said to me, 'Mortal, these bones are the whole house of Israel. They say, 'Our bones are dried up, and our hope is lost; we are cut off completely.'* ¹² Therefore prophesy, and say to them, Thus says the Lord GOD: I am going to open your graves, and bring you up from your graves, O my people; and I will bring you back to the land of Israel. ¹³ And you shall know that I am the LORD, when I open your graves, and bring you up from your graves, O my people. ¹⁴ I will put my spirit within you, and you shall live, and I will place you on your own soil; then you shall know that I, the LORD, have spoken and will act,' says the LORD.

Initial observations

Along with Isaiah and Jeremiah, Ezekiel is one of the major prophets. According to the book itself, the author was a priest who was deported to Babylon in 597 BC. The text is the fruit of penetrating theological reflection on why the disaster of exile befell Israel. Although it does exhibit typical features of prophetic speech, the book is so carefully written, with consistent themes and magnificently elaborate metaphors, that we may view it as a chiefly literary work.

Kind of writing

Ezekiel 37:1–14 is a vision report, in two parts: 1–10 (the oracle) and 11–14 (the interpretation, our reading substantially). Vv. 11–14, like the vision report, are in two parts, one negative (11), the other positive (12–14). The phrase 'says the Lord' acts as a frame around the positive parts.

Origin of the reading

Traditionally, the book was seen to be in two parts: chapters 1–24 (doom) and 25–48 (consolation), not unlike the Book of Jeremiah. Nowadays, scholars notice that the book is shaped by three great visions of God: Ezekiel 1, 8–11, 40–48. A proposed layout looks like this:

Layout of the whole book

1–7	First vision, call, preparation
8–39	Ezekiel among the exiles
40–48	The New Kingdom

Layout of the middle section:

8–11	Temple abominations
12–15	Contra Jerusalem leaders
16–23	Abominations revealed
24–33	YHWH against rebels
24	Jerusalem siege (start)
25–32	Against the nations

33   Jerusalem siege (end)

34–39   *YHWH restores Israel*

Our reading, therefore, comes from that part where the prophet turns to restoration and new life, which is to be developed fully in Ezekiel 40–48.

Related passages

I will take you from the nations, and gather you from all the countries, and bring you into your own land. I will sprinkle clean water upon you, and you shall be clean from all your uncleannesses, and from all your idols I will cleanse you. A new heart I will give you, and a new spirit I will put within you; and I will remove from your body the heart of stone and give you a heart of flesh. I will put my spirit within you, and make you follow my statutes and be careful to observe my ordinances. Then you shall live in the land that I gave to your ancestors; and you shall be my people, and I will be your God. (Ezekiel 36:24–28)

Brief commentary

(V.11)
The divine voice speaks again (see vv. 3, 4 and 9). A corporate interpretation is given to the symbolic discourse. In the threefold lament, we overhear the searing complaint of the exiles. 'We are cut off' means we have experienced death. Bitter experience has sapped the life out of them.

(Vv. 12–13)
Building on the gruesome images of revived corpses in vv. 1–10, the prophet offers a plain meaning: the return and restoration of Israel. The Exile was experienced as a graveyard for the people; correspondingly, the return from Exile is portrayed as a resurrection. Notice how the triple lament is matched by a threefold offer of salvation. In this new exodus, God saves Israel again. Even more importantly, God reveals his true self. In Ezekiel, salvation is a means to an end, the unveiling of God. Thus, at its heart, redemption *by* God is a revelation *of* God. (Likewise, the raising of Lazarus tells us who Jesus is.)

(V. 14)

The strong conclusion ties the interpretation to the oracle in vv.1–10, but also links with earlier equally significant affirmations about the new heart and the new spirit (see above, Ezekiel 36:24–28). The nine repetitions of breath/spirit in 37:1–4 should also be kept in mind. This makes our reference here the ninth, climactic affirmation. While not always clear in translations, the Hebrew word for breath/spirit – *rûah* – is used throughout.

Ezekiel does speak of national restoration, making metaphorical use of resurrection. It may be presumed that this made sense to his audience, reflecting some conviction about life after death.

Pointers for prayer

a) There is a lament at the start of the reading, a real cry from the heart. Does it resonate with any happenings in my own life?

b) The words of Julian of Norwich come to mind: all shall be well, and all shall be well and all manner of thing shall be well. Faith alone helps.

Prayer

God of all life, we are in your hands and into your hands we commend our spirit, our life, our all. Strengthen us when we feel all hope is gone and let us know your presence in our lives. Through Christ our Lord. Amen.

Themes across the readings

Our first reading is not really about personal resurrection. Nevertheless, it affirms faith in God who has power over death and life. It names something of the tragedy of the human condition and God's responding offer of salvation.

Ezekiel's promise of a new heart and a new spirit finds an echo in Paul's great chapter 8 to the Romans: the link between the Spirit of him who raised Jesus from the dead and our own experience of the indwelling Spirit.

Like the first reading, the Lazarus story names the human condition. What is God's response? The phrase 'see how much he loved love him' is a clue. Only in the Fourth Gospel do we find the teaching that God loves us enough to raise us from the dead. Resurrection is no longer simply a gift or even an event, but a person. Jesus is for us the resurrection and the life.

Chapter 6

Palm Sunday A

Thought for the day

Official memorial celebrations are familiar to us, marking wars or national events. Often, these are coloured by a mixture of sadness and gratitude. The Christian memorial of the last week of Jesus' life is entirely different. First of all, we tell the whole story again *because he is risen from the dead.* Secondly, this memorial is an *effective* one: as we do this in memory of him, the very same gifts of compassion, forgiveness, love and healing are offered again to all present, precisely because Jesus *is risen from the dead.* Our Christian memory is not a dead remembering but an *effective* bringing into the present of the great events that gave us new life in Christ.

Prayer

Saving God, as we recall in word and gesture the great events of salvation, let us know your healing love once more. Through Christ our Lord. Amen.

Gospel

The Passion is quite long (Matthew 26:14–27:66), so only the central paragraphs are given here. Of course, it should all be read.

> **Mt 27:32** As they went out, they came upon a man from Cyrene named Simon; they compelled this man to carry his cross. ³³ And when they came to a place called Golgotha

(which means Place of a Skull), ³⁴ they offered him wine to drink, mixed with gall; but when he tasted it, he would not drink it. ³⁵ And when they had crucified him, they divided his clothes among themselves by casting lots; ³⁶ then they sat down there and kept watch over him. ³⁷ Over his head they put the charge against him, which read, 'This is Jesus, the King of the Jews.'

Mt 27:38 Then two bandits were crucified with him, one on his right and one on his left. ³⁹ Those who passed by derided him, shaking their heads ⁴⁰ and saying, 'You who would destroy the temple and build it in three days, save yourself! If you are the Son of God, come down from the cross.' ⁴¹ In the same way the chief priests also, along with the scribes and elders, were mocking him, saying, ⁴² 'He saved others; he cannot save himself. He is the King of Israel; let him come down from the cross now, and we will believe in him. ⁴³ He trusts in God; let God deliver him now, if he wants to; for he said, 'I am God's Son.'" ⁴⁴ The bandits who were crucified with him also taunted him in the same way.

Mt 27:45 From noon on, darkness came over the whole land until three in the afternoon. ⁴⁶ And about three o'clock Jesus cried with a loud voice, 'Eli, Eli, lama sabachthani?' that is, 'My God, my God, why have you forsaken me?' ⁴⁷ When some of the bystanders heard it, they said, 'This man is calling for Elijah.' ⁴⁸ At once one of them ran and got a sponge, filled it with sour wine, put it on a stick, and gave it to him to drink. ⁴⁹ But the others said, 'Wait, let us see whether Elijah will come to save him.' ⁵⁰ Then Jesus cried again with a loud voice and breathed his last. ⁵¹ At that moment the curtain of the temple was torn in two, from top to bottom. The earth shook, and the rocks were split. ⁵² The tombs also were opened, and many bodies of the saints who had fallen asleep were raised. ⁵³ After his resurrection they came out of the tombs and entered the holy city and appeared to many. ⁵⁴ Now when the centurion and those with him, who were keeping watch over Jesus, saw the earthquake and what took place, they were terrified and said, 'Truly this man was God's Son!'

Mt 27:55 Many women were also there, looking on from a distance; they had followed Jesus from Galilee and had provided for him. [56] Among them were Mary Magdalene, and Mary the mother of James and Joseph, and the mother of the sons of Zebedee.

Mt 27:57 When it was evening, there came a rich man from Arimathea, named Joseph, who was also a disciple of Jesus.

Initial observations

There is a core similarity between the four accounts of the death of Jesus in the New Testament. However, they differ in sequence and in details, allowing various understandings of the cross to unfold. Thus both Mark and Matthew treat the death as tragedy, the tragic outcome of the ministry of Jesus, rejected by his people and abandoned by his followers. Luke, in contrast, treats the death of Jesus as that of a martyr-prophet, on the model of Old Testament prophets, who suffered for their preaching and in anticipation of the death of Stephen in the Acts (by Luke also). In the Fourth Gospel, the portrayal is that of a triumph, which brings together the lifting up, the honour and the glorification of Jesus. Because the death of Jesus was and is such a deeply mysterious and indeed perplexing event, different dimensions are explored and laid bare by different New Testament writers, the earliest being Paul.

Kind of writing

The scenes recounted belong to the genre of biography, dealing with the tragic end of Jesus' ministry. Using narrative 'adjustments', each Gospel writer offers his own interpretation.

Old Testament background

(i) In all the accounts, there is an underlay of reference to the Psalms and the Prophets. By delving into the Hebrew Bible, the first generation of Christians hoped to understand what had happened on the cross as somehow in continuity with God's earlier word. Psalm 22, in italics below, is especially rich in resonance.

Psalm 69:21: They gave me poison for food, and for my thirst they gave me vinegar to drink. Psalm 22:18: *They divide my clothes among themselves, and for my clothing they cast lots.* Psalm 22:7: *All who see me mock at me; they make mouths at me, they shake their heads;* Psalm 109:25: I am an object of scorn to my accusers; when they see me, they shake their heads. Lamentations 2:15: All who pass along the way clap their hands at you; they hiss and wag their heads at the daughter of Jerusalem; 'Is this the city that was called the perfection of beauty, the joy of all the earth?' Psalm 22:8: *'Commit your cause to the Lord; let him deliver – let him rescue the one in whom he delights!'* Wisdom 2:18: for if the righteous man is God's child, he will help him, and will deliver him from the hand of his adversaries. [19] Let us test him with insult and torture, so that we may find out how gentle he is, and make trial of his forbearance. [20] Let us condemn him to a shameful death, for, according to what he says, he will be protected.' Amos 8:9: On that day, says the Lord God, I will make the sun go down at noon, and darken the earth in broad daylight. Psalm 22:1: *My God, my God, why have you forsaken me? Why are you so far from helping me, from the words of my groaning?*

Ezekiel 37:12: Therefore prophesy, and say to them, Thus says the Lord God: I am going to open your graves, and bring you up from your graves, O my people; and I will bring you back to the land of Israel. Deuteronomy 21:22: When someone is convicted of a crime punishable by death and is executed, and you hang him on a tree, [23] his corpse must not remain all night upon the tree; you shall bury him that same day, for anyone hung on a tree is under God's curse. You must not defile the land that the Lord your God is giving you for possession.

(ii) An especially rich resource for early Christian reflection were the Suffering Servant Songs in Isaiah (42:1–4; 49:1–6; 50:4–9 and 52:13–53:12). In the historical context the Servant is, perhaps, Israel. The early Christians saw here passages that helped them come to grips with the crucifixion. The links are as follows:

First Song: Isaiah 42:1–4; Mt 12:18

Second Song: Isaiah 49:1–6: Mt 12:18

Third Song: Isaiah 50:4–9; Mt 5:39

Fourth Song: Isaiah 52:13–53:12. See below for the detailed reference.

> Surely he has borne our infirmities and carried our diseases; yet we accounted him stricken, struck down by God, and afflicted. (Isaiah 53:4 = *Mt 8:17*)

> He was oppressed, and he was afflicted, yet he did not open his mouth; like a lamb that is led to the slaughter, and like a sheep that before its shearers is silent, so he did not open his mouth. (Isaiah 53:7 = *Mt 26:63*)

> Yet it was the will of the LORD to crush him with pain. When you make his life an offering for sin, he shall see his offspring, and shall prolong his days; through him the will of the LORD shall prosper. Out of his anguish he shall see light; he shall find satisfaction through his knowledge. The righteous one, my servant, shall make many righteous, and he shall bear their iniquities. Therefore I will allot him a portion with the great, and he shall divide the spoil with the strong; because he poured out himself to death, and was numbered with the transgressors; yet he bore the sin of many, and made intercession for the transgressors. (Isaiah 53:10–12 = *Mt 20:28; for v. 12 see all Mt 26:28, 27:38*)

New Testament foreground

(i) The Passion Predictions help us see the theology of the writer and, perhaps, something of the understanding of Jesus himself: Matthew 16:21; 17:22; 20:17–19.

(ii) The words at the Supper also interpret the death: Matthew 26:26–29.

(iii) Earthquakes are introduced to indicate God's presence and action.

St Paul

For as often as you eat this bread and drink the cup, you proclaim the Lord's death until he comes. (1 Corinthians 11:26)

Brief commentary

(V. 32)
Simon, a historical figure, here models authentic discipleship: Matthew 10:37–39; 16:24–28.

(V. 37)
Cruelly ironic in the light of the rejection at 27:25.

(V. 39)
A combination of the important temple saying with the temptations at the beginning of the ministry. Jesus confronts evil as such.

(V. 45)
Symbolic darkness, signalling that the cross is an end-time event.

(V. 46)
The first words of Psalm 22, placing the death of Jesus in the context of a psalm of lament, which itself returns at the end to deep confidence in God.

(V. 47)

Elijah was expected at the end (Malachi 4:5); his mention tells us that something to do with God's final, end-time purpose is unfolding here.

(V. 50)

The actual death is a wordless cry.

(Vv. 51f.)

The curtain stands for the mother religion of Judaism, represented by the curtain which veiled God's presence. The earthquake is symbolic. Matthew, Luke and John bring the consequences of the death forward in a symbolic way.

(V. 54)

A profound Gentile confession, matching Peter's at Matthew 16:13ff.

(V. 55)

The women at a distance contrast with the women in John 19. Some of them will be witness to the resurrection (see Matthew 27:61).

(V. 57)

Probably a historical recollection; the burial is dignified and matter-of-fact.

Pointers for prayer

The account of the Passion is a vivid story with a variety of characters and much action. To enter into the passage we can read the story slowly and see if we can identify with different characters in the story. Any one scene within the story can provide us with much food for reflection and prayer. Keep in mind that one of the aims in reflecting on the passage is to discover the GOOD NEWS the story has for us. Here are just a few general pointers for prayer.

a) The identity of Jesus is revealed as the Messiah and the Son of God, not with a display of human power, but as one who was prepared to suffer unto death to show us how our God loves us. How does the Passion story speak to you as a revelation of how God loves you?

b) Jesus gives us an example of patient endurance and faithfulness in suffering. Suffering is something we all encounter. It is not something that anyone likes but sometimes we cope with it better than others. What have you found helps you to cope better with suffering?

c) As you read through the narrative of the Passion where do you find yourself resonating with a character in the action? Is there any message there for you that is life-giving?

Prayer

O God of eternal glory, you anointed Jesus your servant to bear our sins, to encourage the weary, to raise up and restore the fallen. Keep before our eyes the splendour of the paschal mystery of Christ and, by our sharing in the passion and resurrection, seal our lives with the victorious sign of his obedience and exaltation.

We ask this through Christ, our liberator from sin, who lives with you in the unity of the Holy Spirit, holy and mighty God for ever and ever. Amen.

Second Reading

Phil 2:5 *Let the same mind be in you that was in Christ Jesus,* ⁶ who, though he was in the form of God, did not regard equality with God as something to be exploited, ⁷ but emptied himself, taking the form of a slave, being born in human likeness. And being found in human form, ⁸ he humbled himself and became obedient to the point of death – even death on a cross.

Phil 2:9 Therefore God also highly exalted him and gave him the name that is above every name, ¹⁰ so that at the name of Jesus every knee should bend, in heaven and on earth and under the earth, ¹¹ and every tongue should confess that Jesus Christ is Lord, to the glory of God the Father.

Initial observations

Where did Paul get his information on the Christian tradition? Even before his encounter with Christ, he knew the basics of what the Christians were saying. No doubt the time in Damascus included a great deal of initiation. In the undisputed letters we find traces of acclamation, credal formulae and hymns. Of these hymns, none is more famous than our reading today.

Kind of writing

Philippians is a real letter, with the following outline:

1:1–2	*Letter opening*
1:3–11	Thanksgiving
1:12–26	Paul's own story
1:27–2:16	*Exhortations*
2:17–3:1a	Paul's own story
3:1b–4:9	Exhortations
4:10–20	Thanksgiving
4:21–23	Letter conclusion

Our passage comes from the first set of exhortations and the whole section should be read to see why and how Paul makes use of the hymn at this point.

Context in the community

The letter is addressed to the first Christian community founded by Paul in Europe. The letter mentions that Paul was in prison. The identification of the locations also determines the date: Ephesus (54–55), Caesarea (57–59), Rome (60–61). The occasion of writing is to express gratitude for the gift sent with Epaphroditus. There are several practical issues. Overall, the letter is very personal, with a good deal of autobiography and great deal of affection for the Philippians. There are issues about conduct and behaviour, which bear directly on the use of the hymn.

Related passages

More than that, I regard everything as loss because of the surpassing value of knowing Christ Jesus my Lord. For his sake I have suffered the loss of all things, and I regard them as rubbish, in order that I may gain Christ and be found in him, not having a righteousness of my own that comes from the law, but one that comes through faith in Christ, the righteousness from God based on faith. I want to know Christ and the power of his resurrection and the sharing of his sufferings by becoming like him in his death, if somehow I may attain the resurrection from the dead. (Philippians 3:8–11)

Let those of us then who are mature be of the same mind; and if you think differently about anything, this too God will reveal to you. Only let us hold fast to what we have attained. (Philippians 3:15–16)

For you know the generous act of our Lord Jesus Christ, that though he was rich, yet for your sakes he became poor, so that by his poverty you might become rich. (2 Corinthians 8:9)

But what does it say? 'The word is near you, on your lips and in your heart' (that is, the word of faith that we proclaim); because if you confess with your lips that Jesus is Lord and believe in your heart that God raised him from the dead, you will be saved. (Romans 10:8–9)

Brief commentary

The overall pattern in the hymn is pre-existence, existence and post-existence. Given that the hymn in non-Pauline, it may represent early Christian worship.

(V. 5)
The introduction 'stitches' the hymn into the ethical persuasion. 'Mind'

in Greek is really the verb to think. A good parallel in Paul would be Romans 12:3.

(V. 6)

Form (*morphē*) is difficult. Current in classical and Hellenistic Greek, with a wide range of meanings – 'stature, form, condition, feature, external appearance, reproduction' – *morphē* is used relatively little in the Bible. Exploited is also difficult: It may mean not only 'to grasp something forcefully which one does not have,' but also 'to retain by force what one possesses.' Thus, it is possible to translate 2:6 in two quite different ways.

(V. 7)

'Emptied' in relation to the cross comes up in 1 Corinthians 1:17. Again, the form – *morphē* – of a slave.

(V. 8)

Humble is found in the teaching of Jesus (Matthew 18:4; 23:12; Luke 3:5; 14:11; 18:14). Obedient to death – cf. Hebrews 2:10–18. V. 8c could be an addition by Paul, reflecting his own emphasis on the cross (Philippians 1:29, 3:10, 18 and 1 Corinthians 1:23; 2:2).

(V. 9)

Exalted: the simple form is found in John and Luke–Acts to refer to the resurrection (John 3:14; 8:28; 12:32, 34; Acts 2:33; 5:31). The complex form is found here in the New Testament and in the Greek Old Testament (LXX) only once: 'For you, O Lord, are most high over all the earth; you are exalted far above all gods.' (LXX Psalm 96:9)

(V. 10)

There is a suggestion that this verse may be a liturgical instruction.

(V. 11)

Confess (*homologeō*) is a foundational Christian word, both as verb and as noun (Matthew 7:23; 10:32; 14:7; Luke 12:8; John 1:20; 9:22; 12:42; Acts 7:17; 23:8; 24:14 etc.)

Pointers for prayer

a) Working and living with others is always difficult. Even among Christians, the risk is that we 'read' this reality politically and not, like Paul, spiritually, that is as part of discipleship.

b) Jesus emptied himself: perhaps I have known people like that myself or have been called myself to some extraordinary generosity.

c) When I did I first say 'Jesus is Lord' and mean it from the heart?

Prayer

On the path of discipleship, you call us, loving God, to follow and imitate your Son.

Give to us the generosity to give our all, to lose our lives, that we may be true followers of Jesus, who made himself poor that we might be rich. Through Christ our Lord. Amen.

🌿 First Reading 🌿

Is 50:4 The Lord God has given me the tongue of a teacher, that I may know how to sustain the weary with a word. Morning by morning he wakens – wakens my ear to listen as those who are taught. ⁵ The Lord God has opened my ear, and I was not rebellious, I did not turn backward. ⁶ I gave my back to those who struck me, and my cheeks to those who pulled out the beard; I did not hide my face from insult and spitting. ⁷ The Lord God helps me; therefore I have not been disgraced; therefore I have set my face like flint, and I know that I shall not be put to shame. ⁸ *He who vindicates me is near. Who will contend with me? Let us stand up together. Who are my adversaries? Let them confront me.* ⁹ *It is the Lord God who helps* *me; who will declare me guilty? All of them will wear out like a garment; the moth will eat them up.*

Initial observations

There are four so-called 'Suffering Servant Songs' taken from the prophet known to scholarship as Second Isaiah: 42:1–4; 49:1–6; 50:4–9; 52:13–53:12. The most substantial of these poems is the last one, read in its entirety on Good Friday. The verses omitted by the lectionary are included here to complete the poem.

Kind of writing

This is poetry, in which the writer responds to the sufferings of Israel. The images used are always significant and, in these few verses, note the extensive use of the part of the body: tongue, ear, back, cheeks, beard, faces. In contrast to earlier generations, this Israelite has an open ear. This is really a psalm of confidence.

This particular song is notable for its repeated use of the full name of God in a quite emphatic and personal way: 'Lord GOD' translates ădōnāy YHWH (Lord Yahweh).

Origin of the reading

Isaiah 40–55 comes from teachings proclaimed towards the end of the great Exile in Babylon, when hope of homecoming and return was beginning to dawn. The exile was understood in part to be a consequence of infidelity on the part of the priests and the people. The 'servant' is called upon to undergo the pain of exile in an exemplary fashion so that all Israel can use the bitter experience for spiritual purification.

Related passages

> It is good for one to bear the yoke in youth, ... to give one's cheek to the smiter, and be filled with insults. (Lamentations 3:27, 30)

Brief commentary

(V. 4a)
The prophet pays attention to older prophetic texts and learns from them. Cf. Jeremiah 1:4–10; Is 42:3; 49:5–6. The weary are the disheartened exiles. Teacher = lit. one *taught*. Cf. *Bind up the testimony, seal the teaching among my disciples.* (Isaiah 8:16)

(Vv. 4b–5)
The prophet is fully open to God's word. (Cf. Isaiah 6:10–11; cf. also Isaiah 48 [closed ears])

(V. 6)
In an exemplary fashion, and in contrast to Israel as a whole, the prophet undergoes the just punishment and humiliation. His opponents this time seem to include fellow Israelites (cf. Jeremiah 20:7–13).

(V. 7)
The sufferings of the prophet are endured in view of a later vindication by God. Cf. Ezekiel 3:8–9. He is able to endure because of the help from God.

(V. 8)
The call for a just hearing (a '*riv*') resembles Job at this point, perfectly appropriately. The rhetorical questions are more open than usual.

(V. 9)
God alone vindicates; all human oppression has a sell-by date (using the traditional metaphor of the moth).

Pointers for prayer

a) We are called to be 'hearers of the word,' open to the voice of God. How do I respond, day by day?

b) No one escapes suffering and we all 'deal' with it in different ways. What has my experience been?

c) Has it ever been that some good came from unjust suffering?

Prayer

God of all, we are hearers of the word. On our own path of suffering, give us constant faith in you, the author of all that is good. Through Christ our Lord. Amen.

Chapter 7

Holy Thursday ABC

Thought for the day

The great three days make up a single feast — the 'Triduum' — and present us with the opportunity to live again with 'the great events that gave us new life in Christ.' Tonight's evening Lord's Supper reminds us of the Last Supper and all it would have meant for Jesus himself. The words are simple; the gestures even simpler. Behind the simplicity we see Jesus' fidelity to his Abba, to his identity and to his mission. With bread and wine we mark Jesus' extraordinary journey through death into resurrection, all for love of us. At the heart of it is Jesus' 'yes', a 'yes' to God and a 'yes' to all humanity. *For the Son of God, Jesus Christ, whom we proclaimed among you, Silvanus and Timothy and I, was not 'Yes and No'; but in him it is always 'Yes.' For in him every one of God's promises is a 'Yes.' For this reason it is through him that we say the 'Amen,' to the glory of God.* (2 Corinthians 1:19–20)

Prayer

God of love, may we hear your 'yes' to us all in the 'yes' of Jesus. As we live again his death and resurrection, may our celebration touch our lives and may our 'amen' rise from the depth of our hearts in gratitude, amazement and love. Through Christ our Lord. Amen.

🌿 Gospel 🌿

Jn 13:1 Now before the festival of the Passover, Jesus knew that his hour had come to depart from this world and go to the Father. Having loved his own who were in the world, he loved them to the end. [2] The devil had already put it into the heart of Judas son of Simon Iscariot to betray him. And during supper [3] Jesus, knowing that the Father had given all things into his hands, and that he had come from God and was going to God, [4] got up from the table, took off his outer robe, and tied a towel around himself. [5] Then he poured water into a basin and began to wash the disciples' feet and to wipe them with the towel that was tied around him. [6] He came to Simon Peter, who said to him, 'Lord, are you going to wash my feet?' [7] Jesus answered, 'You do not know now what I am doing, but later you will understand.' [8] Peter said to him, 'You will never wash my feet.' Jesus answered, 'Unless I wash you, you have no share with me.' [9] Simon Peter said to him, 'Lord, not my feet only but also my hands and my head!' [10] Jesus said to him, 'One who has bathed does not need to wash, except for the feet, but is entirely clean. And you are clean, though not all of you.' [11] For he knew who was to betray him; for this reason he said, 'Not all of you are clean.'

[12] After he had washed their feet, had put on his robe, and had returned to the table, he said to them, 'Do you know what I have done to you? [13] You call me Teacher and Lord – and you are right, for that is what I am. [14] So if I, your Lord and Teacher, have washed your feet, you also ought to wash one another's feet. [15] For I have set you an example, that you also should do as I have done to you.'

Initial observations

(i) The Fourth Gospel is in two parts, John 1–12 and John 13–21. The Holy Thursday reading serves a double function: to begin the Book of Glory in a highly solemn way (with vv.1–4) and to begin the story of the Passion with the Last Supper (vv. 5–15).

(ii) The washing of the feet is found only in the Fourth Gospel.

It may draw its inspiration from the Synoptic tradition (see under New Testament Foreground below) but the vocabulary and interpretation are entirely Johannine.

(iii)In the Fourth Gospel – remarkably – there is no account of the Lord's Supper during the Last Supper. This much may be said: looking forward historically, the Lord's Supper interprets the death of death by means of prophetic gesture. In this Gospel, the washing of the feet fulfils exactly the same function (see below for details).

(iv)Finally, we notice the heading 'before the festival of the Passover'. This alerts us to the fact that in this Gospel, the Last Supper is not a Passover meal. According to the Johannine calendar, the Passover that year was Friday night through Saturday. Jesus as the Christian Passover is a significant layer in this Gospel (see 1:29; 19:29; 19:33–36).

Kind of writing

There are three moments here.

(i)   Vv. 1–4 form a solemn introduction or exordium.

(ii) Vv. 5–11 The story falls into a recognisable category from prophetic writings, that of 'prophetic gesture'. Across the Hebrew Bible, but especially in the prophetic books, we find 'prophetic gestures'. These were mini dramas, which vividly illustrated the message of a particular prophet. Of the many examples, here are some from Ezekiel: Ezekiel made a model of Jerusalem – Ezekiel 4:1–3; the rationed food – Ezekiel 4:9–19; the hair – Ezekiel 5; the exile's baggage – Ezekiel 12:1–16; Ezekiel's 'non-bereavement' – Ezekiel 24:15–27.

(iii)Vv. 12–15 form an exhortation, drawing out some of the meaning of the passage.

Old Testament background

Passover is already indicated in the first reading for this liturgy. Another important background is found in prophetic gestures.

New Testament foreground

(i) A dispute also arose among them as to which one of them was to be regarded as the greatest. But he said to them, 'The kings of the Gentiles lord it over them; and those in authority over them are called benefactors. But not so with you; rather the greatest among you must become like the youngest, and the leader like one who serves. For who is greater, the one who is at the table or the one who serves? Is it not the one at the table? But I am among you as one who serves. (Luke 22:24–27)

(ii) Water: this word has an immense significance in this Gospel from start to finish. It points to the source of salvation in Christ, the event of salvation in lifting up on the cross and the gift of salvation in the heart of the believer. (John 1:26, 31, 33; 2:7, 9; 3:5, 23; 4:7, 10–11, 13–15, 46; 5:7; 7:38; 13:5; 19:34)

(iii) The words used have special reference in this Gospel. In Greek, for example, it does not say he got up from the table but that he rose. Likewise, it does not say in Greek he took off his garment but that he laid down his garment. All the words refer in some way to the death and resurrection.

Rose: thirteen times, almost always in reference to the resurrection of Jesus.

Took off: eighteen times, usually in reference to Jesus' laying down his life.

Wrapped: three times, but the links bring us to the miracle in John 21.

Water: twenty-one times, but the contexts are always illuminating

Washing: thirteen times.

Wipe: three times only.

Feet: fourteen times

'Never':   twelve (lit. 'into eternity' with a special meaning).

Bringing these various strands together, we may summarise as follows. The Washing of the Feet is a prophetic gesture in literary form, inspired by the Synoptic tradition. It is not simply an exemplum of service, leading to a primarily moral teaching.

As a prophetic gesture at the Last Supper, indeed as a prophetic gesture replacing the Lord's Supper, its function is identical to that of the words and actions over the bread and wine: the washing of feet interprets the death of Jesus as an act of loving service. The need to insist on this is best felt by remembering the shock of the crucifixion and the immense difficulty this was for Jews at the time.

This means, for example, that the dialogue with Peter is not really about the washing of the feet, taken literally. On the level of Johannine spirituality, it is really about being able to accept that God-in-Jesus loved humanity to such an extraordinary level that God lovingly served humanity by means of his death on the cross.

St Paul

> If then there is any encouragement in Christ, any consolation from love, any sharing in the Spirit, any compassion and sympathy, make my joy complete: be of the same mind, having the same love, being in full accord and of one mind. Do nothing from selfish ambition or conceit, but in humility regard others as better than yourselves. Let each of you look not to your own interests, but to the interests of others.

> Let the same mind be in you that was in Christ Jesus, who, though he was in the form of God, did not regard equality with God as something to be exploited, but emptied himself, taking the form of a slave, being born in human likeness. And being found in human form, he humbled himself and became obedient to the point of death— even death on a cross. (Philippians 2:1–8)

Brief commentary

(V.1)

There are three Passovers in this Gospel. 'Hour' means the special time of salvation/glorification in the lifting up. 'Depart': because he came and was made flesh. 'Love to the end' means (a) up until the end and (b) perfectly. The latter forms a frame with Jesus' last words in this Gospel: 'it is perfected' (literally).

(V. 2)

Jesus faces not just wickedness but evil as such.

(V. 3)

The reference is to the 'Word made flesh' being 'lifted up'.

(V. 4)

Literally, he rose and laid down – evocative words in this Gospel.

(V. 5)

The Johannine Jesus illustrated the teaching of the historical Jesus on service: 'For the Son of Man came not to be served but to serve, and to give his life as ransom for many.' (Mark 10:45)

(V. 6)

The reversal of roles is shocking; however, the real shock is not the immediate issue of foot washing but that God in Christ served humanity on the cross. This was the crux of the matter for Jews who could not accept Jesus. Cf. Mark 8:31–33 – also on the lips of Peter.

(V. 7)

Understanding later is a commonplace in John's Gospel. This later understanding is a gift of the Spirit. See 2:22; 12:16; 16:12–15.

(V. 8)

The objection is stronger and Jesus' reply is a key: having a share with him in what?

(V. 9)

Feet, hands and head: cf. the treatment of Jesus himself.

(V. 10)
Possibly a reference to baptism at the time of writing.

(V. 11)
This negative, jarring note reminds us immediately of the death of Jesus.

(V. 12)
An open question, taking us behind the simple act of washing.

(V. 13)
Cf. Luke 22:24–27 above.

(V. 14)
Why so concrete? Why not a general principle? Because the cross was concrete and our service too is always particular and practical. Thus, having been serviced by the crucified, we live a cruciform discipleship.

(V. 15)
The little word 'as' (*kathōs*) is vital in this Gospel: 'This is my commandment, that you love one another as I have loved you' (John 15:12). It means more than to follow an example; it means to live from the originating gift.

Pointers for prayer

a) Loving to the end and perfectly – when has that been my experience? Whom am I called to love like that?

b) There is a reversal of roles taking place – illustrating the heart of the Gospel. Have I ever broken the mould of expectation and acted 'out of role'? What gave me courage?

c) Peter finds it hard to be served – sometimes it is easier to give than to receive. When have I hesitated to receive? Do I find it hard to receive from God?

d) There are no ethics as such in the Fourth Gospel – love is all, summarised provocatively by St Augustine: *dilige, et quod vis fac* (love and do what you will).

Prayer

O God, in the fullness of time, you revealed your love in Jesus the Lord. On the eve of his death, as a sign of your covenant, he washed the feet of his disciples and gave himself as food and drink.

Give us life at this sacred banquet and joy in humble service, that, bound to Christ in all things, we may pass over from this world to your kingdom, where he lives and reigns with you now and always in the unity of the Holy Spirit, God for ever and ever. Amen.

🌿 Second Reading 🌿

1 Cor 11:23 For I received from the Lord what I also handed on to you, that the Lord Jesus on the night when he was betrayed took a loaf of bread, [24] and when he had given thanks, he broke it and said, 'This is my body that is for you. Do this in remembrance of me.' [25] In the same way he took the cup also, after supper, saying, 'This cup is the new covenant in my blood. Do this, as often as you drink it, in remembrance of me.' [26] For as often as you eat this bread and drink the cup, you proclaim the Lord's death until he comes.

Initial observations

This is the earliest account of the Lord's Supper to come down to us. Nevertheless, it already shows the marks of liturgical evolution, such as the repeated injunction, 'Do this in memory of me.' Paul has this story as one of the very few incidents in Jesus' life that he recounts.

Kind of writing

This is a tradition report, using some of the technical language of the rabbis. The Last Supper is reported four times in the New Testament, once in each of the Synoptic gospels and here in Paul. Paul's account is the earliest.

Context in the community

The context in the community is strife and division, especially along the lines of rich/poor. It seems clear that the poor members are being disparaged and not properly recognised as equally members of the body of Christ. Paul does offer an immensely practical solution (see below), but behind lies his great theology of the body of Christ.

Related passages

Theological considerations

Whoever, therefore, eats the bread or drinks the cup of the Lord in an unworthy manner will be answerable for the body and blood of the Lord. Examine yourselves, and only then eat of the bread and drink of the cup. For all who eat and drink without discerning the body, eat and drink judgement against themselves. For this reason many of you are weak and ill, and some have died. But if we judged ourselves, we would not be judged. But when we are judged by the Lord, we are disciplined so that we may not be condemned along with the world. (1 Corinthians 11:27–32)

Practical solutions

So then, my brothers and sisters, when you come together to eat, wait for one another. If you are hungry, eat at home, so that when you come together, it will not be for your condemnation. About the other things I will give instructions when I come. (1 Corinthians 11:33–34)

From the Didache
The Didache is interesting because it inverts the order: the wine is first and only then the bread.

And concerning the broken bread: We give you thanks, our Father, for the life and knowledge that you have made known to us through Jesus, your servant; to you be the glory forever.

Just as this broken bread was scattered upon the mountains and then was gathered together and became one, so may your church be gathered together from the ends of the earth into your kingdom; for yours is the glory and the power through Jesus Christ forever. (Didache 9:3–4)

Brief commentary

(V. 23)

Paul used the technical term for handing on Pharisaic traditions. NB a single loaf, because it is not bread in general, so to speak, but the one concrete loaf which counts. Cf. the Didache.

(V. 24)

A prophetic gesture, disclosing to those present the meaning of Jesus' death on the following day.

(V. 25)

The words over the cup recall the covenant, as well as being an echo of the fourth Suffering Servant Song from Isaiah.

(V. 26)

As always, Paul is aware of the tension between the 'already' and the 'not yet' of Christian living. In contrast to the Corinthians, some of whom think everything is now and that is all there is, Paul teaches that the present moment is only a first instalment of what is to come.

Pointers for prayer

a) When have I experienced a truly memorable Eucharist? What made it special? Has the memory of it helped me understand something of every Eucharist?

b) Community is essential to the Eucharist and when that is fractured then the celebration is impaired and its true meaning hindered. This is still true today: community celebrates Eucharist and Eucharist makes community.

Prayer

May familiarity never blind us to the immense riches we have in the Lord's Supper. By our celebration tonight bring us back to a true celebration that we may encounter the Risen Lord in word, sacrament and community. Through Christ our Lord. Amen.

🍃 First Reading 🍃

Ex 12:1 The LORD said to Moses and Aaron in the land of Egypt: ² This month shall mark for you the beginning of months; it shall be the first month of the year for you. ³ Tell the whole congregation of Israel that on the tenth of this month they are to take a lamb for each family, a lamb for each household. ⁴ If a household is too small for a whole lamb, it shall join its closest neighbour in obtaining one; the lamb shall be divided in proportion to the number of people who eat of it. ⁵ Your lamb shall be without blemish, a year-old male; you may take it from the sheep or from the goats. ⁶ You shall keep it until the fourteenth day of this month; then the whole assembled congregation of Israel shall slaughter it at twilight. ⁷ They shall take some of the blood and put it on the two doorposts and the lintel of the houses in which they eat it. ⁸ They shall eat the lamb that same night; they shall eat it roasted over the fire with unleavened bread and bitter herbs. ⁹ Do not eat any of it raw or boiled in water, but roasted over the fire, with its head, legs and inner organs. ¹⁰ You shall let none of it remain until the morning; anything that remains until the morning you shall burn.

¹¹ This is how you shall eat it: your loins girded, your sandals on your feet, and your staff in your hand; and you shall eat it hurriedly. It is the passover of the LORD. ¹² For I will pass through the land of Egypt that night, and I will strike down every firstborn in the land of Egypt, both human beings and animals; on all the gods of Egypt I will execute judgments: I am the LORD. ¹³ The blood shall be a sign for you on the houses where you live: when I see the blood, I will pass over

you, and no plague shall destroy you when I strike the land of Egypt.

Ex 12:14 This day shall be a day of remembrance for you. You shall celebrate it as a festival to the LORD; throughout your generations you shall observe it as a perpetual ordinance.

Initial observations

It is quite likely that the Last Supper was not, in fact, a Passover meal, and that the timing in the Fourth Gospel is more accurate. (In the Fourth Gospel, the Passover occurs on the Friday night of the same week.) Nevertheless, it was in Passover week, and the feast is indeed part of the context. In that sense, the first reading is the obvious one to read today.

Kind of writing

This is a narrative that supports and explains a ritual practice. The best commentary for the *function* of the ritual may come not from the Bible but from the Mishnah, where the explanation is very close to our practice of the Eucharist. There we read:

> In every generation a person is duty-bound to regard himself as if he personally has gone forth from Egypt, since it is said, And you shall tell your son in that day saying, it is because of that which the Lord did for me when I came forth out of Egypt (Exodus 13:8). Therefore we are duty-bound to thank, praise, glorify, honour, exalt, extol and bless him who did for our forefathers and for us all these miracles. He brought us forth from slavery to freedom, anguish to joy, mourning to festival, darkness to great light, subjugation to redemption, so we should say before him, Hallelujah. (Mishnah Pesahim 10:5)

Origin of the reading

This passage reflects a long history, with the final shape reflecting later Passover practices.

The origins of what became the Passover may go back to agrarian spring fertility rites, offerings of the first fruits of the flocks and of the crops (nomadic/settled). These practices were then linked then to the Exodus and ever after as a memorial or *zikkron*.

Related passages

So Moses told the Israelites that they should keep the passover. They kept the passover in the first month, on the fourteenth day of the month, at twilight, in the wilderness of Sinai. Just as the LORD had commanded Moses, so the Israelites did. Now there were certain people who were unclean through touching a corpse, so that they could not keep the passover on that day. (Numbers 9:4–6)

Brief commentary

The telling combines ritual details, practicalities and a kind of allegorical interpretation. The reading reflects the practices of early Judaism, by which time the Passover had become *the* pilgrimage feast.

Pointers for prayer

a) Memory – as we know sadly from its loss – has tremendous power for maintaining both identity and hope. Can you recall any particular memories that sustained you when times were difficult?

b) In this reading, the sense of anticipated liberation is powerful. In our Christian exodus and Passover, we too are set free – set free *from* and set free *for*.

Prayer

We praise you, loving God, for your many gifts: gift of love, hope and liberation. Help us to embrace the freedom you offer and to keep it alive by the good choices that we make. Through Christ our Lord. Amen.

Chapter 8

Good Friday ABC

Thought for the day

At the centre of our faith stand 'the great events that give us new life in Christ'. How these events have been understood has naturally changed over time, depending on experience, culture and the questions being asked at any particular time. Traditionally, redemption (lit. buying back) was completed once Jesus had died. The Fourth Gospel is very helpful in this regard because it does not separate the death from the resurrection. John uses a single expression to convey the one integrated saving event: the lifting up. At its heart, this is a therapeutic metaphor taken from the story of Moses and the bronze serpent.

Prayer

Saving God, we are all in need of your healing in Christ. Send us again your gifts of forgiveness, victory over death and freedom from fear. Through Christ our Lord. Amen.

❧ Gospel ❧

The full passion is quite long (John 18:1–19:42). Here we produce the centre of the drama and its dénouement, vv. 16b–42. It should, of course, all be read for reflection and prayer.

Jn 19:16b So they took Jesus; [17] and carrying the cross by himself, he went out to what is called The Place of the Skull, which in Hebrew is called Golgotha. [18] There they crucified him, and with him two others, one on either side, with Jesus between them. [19] Pilate also had an inscription written and put on the cross. It read, 'Jesus of Nazareth, the King of the Jews'. [20] Many of the Jews read this inscription, because the place where Jesus was crucified was near the city; and it was written in Hebrew, in Latin and in Greek. [21] Then the chief priests of the Jews said to Pilate, 'Do not write, "The King of the Jews",but, "This man said, I am King of the Jews."' [22] Pilate answered, 'What I have written I have written.' [23] When the soldiers had crucified Jesus, they took his clothes and divided them into four parts, one for each soldier. They also took his tunic; now the tunic was seamless, woven in one piece from the top. [24] So they said to one another, 'Let us not tear it, but cast lots for it to see who will get it.' This was to fulfill what the scripture says,

'They divided my clothes among themselves,
and for my clothing they cast lots.'
[25] And that is what the soldiers did.

Meanwhile, standing near the cross of Jesus were his mother, and his mother's sister, Mary the wife of Clopas, and Mary Magdalene. [26] When Jesus saw his mother and the disciple whom he loved standing beside her, he said to his mother, 'Woman, here is your son.' [27] Then he said to the disciple, 'Here is your mother.' And from that hour the disciple took her into his own home.

Jn 19:28 After this, when Jesus knew that all was now finished, he said (in order to fulfil the scripture), 'I am thirsty.' [29] A jar full of sour wine was standing there. So they put a sponge full of the wine on a branch of hyssop and held it to his mouth. [30] When Jesus had received the wine, he said, 'It is finished.' Then he bowed his head and gave up his spirit.

Jn 19:31 Since it was the day of Preparation, the Jews did not want the bodies left on the cross during the sabbath, especially because that sabbath was a day of great solemnity. So they asked Pilate to have the legs of the crucified men broken and the bodies removed. [32] Then the soldiers came and broke the legs of the first and of the other who had been crucified with him. [33] But when they came to Jesus and saw that he was already dead, they did not break his legs. [34] Instead, one of the soldiers pierced his side with a spear, and at once blood and water came out. [35] (He who saw this has testified so that you also may believe. His testimony is true, and he knows that he tells the truth.) [36] These things occurred so that the scripture might be fulfilled, 'None of his bones shall be broken.' [37] And again another passage of scripture says, 'They will look on the one whom they have pierced.'

Jn 19:38 After these things, Joseph of Arimathea, who was a disciple of Jesus, though a secret one because of his fear of the Jews, asked Pilate to let him take away the body of Jesus. Pilate gave him permission; so he came and removed his body. [39] Nicodemus, who had at first come to Jesus by night, also came, bringing a mixture of myrrh and aloes, weighing about a hundred pounds. [40] They took the body of Jesus and wrapped it with the spices in linen cloths, according to the burial custom of the Jews. [41] Now there was a garden in the place where he was crucified, and in the garden there was a new tomb in which no one had ever been laid. [42] And so, because it was the Jewish day of Preparation, and the tomb was nearby, they laid Jesus there.

Initial observations

All the accounts of Jesus' death tell fundamentally the same story. However, the details vary considerably and are highly significant. It is not just a question of what people remembered. The added stories and words consistently reflect the understanding each Gospel writer offers of the meaning of the cross and resurrection.

Kind of writing

This is a combination of a fundamentally historical narrative enriched with symbolic details to carry the interpretation of the evangelist. The primary frames in this Gospel are therapeutic (the lifting up of the Son of Man) and new creation.

New Testament foreground

> On the third day there was a wedding in Cana of Galilee, and the mother of Jesus was there. (John 2:1)

> Simon Peter and another disciple followed Jesus. Since that disciple was known to the high priest, he went with Jesus into the courtyard of the high priest, but Peter was standing outside at the gate. So the other disciple, who was known to the high priest, went out, spoke to the woman who guarded the gate, and brought Peter in. (John 18:15–16)

> One of his disciples – the one whom Jesus loved – was reclining next to him; Simon Peter therefore motioned to him to ask Jesus of whom he was speaking. (John 13:23–25)

Old Testament background

(i) New Creation: In the beginning when God created the heavens and the earth, the earth was a formless void and darkness covered the face of the deep, while a wind from God swept over the face of the waters. (Genesis 1:1–3) And on the seventh day God finished the work that he had done, and he rested on the seventh day from all the work that he had done. So God blessed the seventh day and hallowed it, because on it God rested from all the work that he had done in creation. (Genesis 2:2–3)

(ii) Psalms: On you I was cast from my birth, and since my mother bore me you have been my God. (Psalm 22:10) I can count all my bones. They stare and gloat over me; they divide my clothes among themselves, and for my clothing they cast lots. (Psalm 22:17–18) They gave me poison for food, and for my thirst they gave me vinegar to drink. (Psalm 69:21)

(iii) Passover: Take a bunch of hyssop, dip it in the blood that is in the basin, and touch the lintel and the two doorposts with the blood in the basin. None of you shall go outside the door of your house until morning. (Exodus 12:22) It shall be eaten in one house; you shall not take any of the animal outside the house, and you shall not break any of its bones. (Exodus 12:46)

St Paul

For it is the God who said, 'Let light shine out of darkness,' who has shone in our hearts to give the light of the knowledge of the glory of God in the face of Jesus Christ. (2 Corinthians 4:6)

So if anyone is in Christ, there is a new creation: everything old has passed away; see, everything has become new! (2 Corinthians 5:17)

For neither circumcision nor uncircumcision is anything; but a new creation is everything! (Galatians 6:15)

Brief commentary

Because there is much to say in a brief space, the commentary is offered by paragraph rather than by verse.

(i) 17–25a Discussion [with Pilate]

In this Gospel, Jesus always uses 'lifted up' to refer to his death (John 3:14; 8:28; 13:32, 34). Simon of Cyrene is important in the other Gospels and surely historical. Here, however, he is deleted on account of John 10:17 and 17:19. Psalm 22:16 is explicitly cited (cf. John 10:8).

Three languages evoke commerce, culture and religion and point to something international or, better, universal taking place. Nazareth: Jesus' birthplace is a subject of dispute else where in this Gospel (John 1:46; 7:41; 7:52).

(ii) 25b–27 Mother and Beloved Disciple

One for each soldier: headdress, cloak, belt and shoes (i.e. four soldiers). Instead of underlining the mockery of the soldiers, John underlines their unwitting fulfilment of scripture – Psalm 22:18. Because Mary is not named in this Gospel ('mother' and 'woman') and because she is not mentioned as being present in the other Gospels, a metaphorical or spiritual interpretation is called for. Taking inspiration from the wedding feast of Cana, the mother or woman is symbolic of the daughter of Zion. Likewise, the beloved disciple (absent in Mark, Matthew and Luke) is symbolic of ideal discipleship. The words have a deeper meaning: an appeal to mother Judaism to recognise the legitimacy of her offspring, Christianity, and an appeal to Christianity to recognise the continued maternity of Judaism. 'Hour' – a seemingly harmless time maker – has a tremendous spiritual and theological resonance in this Gospel (John 1:39; 2:4; 4:6, 21, 23, 52; 5:25, 28, 35; 7:30; 8:20; 11:9; 12:23, 27; 13:1; 16:2, 4, 21, 25, 32; 17:1; 19:14 and, finally, here in 19:17). The cross-references in John are always illuminating.

(iii) 28–30 Death of Jesus

'Finished' frames the scene. 'Finish' could also be translated 'perfected' as in John 13:1. 'Vinegar' is an echo of Psalm 69:21. 'I thirst' picks up Psalm 63:1 (cf. John 4:7). See also John 18:11. 'Hyssop': in the other Gospels 'stick' is used. John specifies hyssop here because of Numbers 19:18 and Exodus 12:22 (cf. Hebrews 9:19). 'Finished'/'perfected' also takes up Genesis 2:2. Cf. In the beginning in John 1:1 and Genesis 1:1. 'Handing over the spirit (pneuma)' is likewise unusual. It is interesting to note that the Synoptics usually avoid using the ordinary terms for the dying of Jesus (*apothneskō* and *teleutaō*):

Mark and Luke: he expired (*exepneusen*)

> Matthew: he let his spirit depart (*apheken to pneuma*)
> John: he handed over his spirit (*paredoken to pneuma*)

This 'handing over' matches the words of the Risen Lord in the next chapter: 'receive the Holy Spirit.' Cf. John 7:39; 16:7; 20:22.

(iv) 31–37 Discussion with Pilate

The non-breaking of the legs is yet another piece of Passover symbolism as in Exodus 12:46; Numbers 9:12; Psalm 34:20. Blood: the single reference here resumes the few but powerful uses earlier in the Gospel: John 1:13 and 6:53–56. This Gospel is awash with water symbolism: apart from the reference here, we are meant to recall as well the following occurrences: 1:26, 31, 33; 2:6–7, 9; 3:5, 23; 4:7, 10–15, 28, 46; 5:7 and, especially, 7:38 and 13:5.

The word 'pierced' is meant as an echo of Zechariah 12:10 (also picked up by Revelation 1:7).

And I will pour out a spirit of compassion and supplication on the house of David and the inhabitants of Jerusalem, so that, when they look on the one whom they have pierced, they shall mourn for him, as one mourns for an only child, and weep bitterly over him, as one weeps over a firstborn. (Zechariah 12:10)

(v) 38–42 'Royal' Burial

Joseph of Arimathea suddenly appears and he is likely to be historical. Nicodemus appears for the third and final time, perhaps representing the more difficult journey of the Pharisee to faith. What about aloes and myrrh? Interestingly, the *binomium* occurs only in Psalm 45:8, Proverbs 7:17 and Songs 4:14, always in the context of nuptial symbolism. In a very indirect way, the writer takes us back to the nuptial symbolism from John 2–4. 'Garden' is an echo of Eden and an anticipation of the 'gardener' in John 20.

Pointers for prayer

a) 'The Good Shepherd lays down his life' (John 10). What has been my experience of being loved? Who has made sacrifices for me? Do these human experiences help me approach the death of Jesus, for me? Prayer of being loved.

b) 'God so loved the world' (John 3). The leap of faith in the cross and resurrection is not so much to believe a doctrine but to trust God, as God of living. What is my experience of trust and being trusted? Prayer of faith and love.

c) 'This is the Lamb of God' (John 1). Jesus' death sets us free. How am I unfree? Have I ever experienced release? Who helped me? What was it like? To what in me is the Risen Jesus speaking a word of liberation today?

d) There was always God's Spirit in the world. Yet, after Jesus' death and resurrection the role of the Spirit has so changed that we can speak of a new gift of the Spirit. What is my own experience of 'before and after' events? What have been the 'before and after' events in my life as a believer?

Prayer

From the throne of grace, O God of mercy,
hear the devout prayer of your people.

As your Son is lifted high upon the cross, draw into his exalted life all who are reborn in the blood and water flowing from his opened side.

We ask this through Jesus Christ, our Passover and our peace, who lives and reigns with you in the unity of the Holy Spirit, holy and mighty God, for ever and ever. Amen.

🌿 Second Reading 🌿

Heb 4:14 Since, then, we have a great high priest who has passed through the heavens, Jesus, the Son of God, let us hold fast to our confession. [15] For we do not have a high priest who is unable to sympathise with our weaknesses, but we have one who in every respect has been tested as we are, yet without sin. [16] Let us therefore approach the throne of grace with boldness, so that we may receive mercy and find grace to help in time of need.

Heb 5:7 In the days of his flesh, Jesus offered up prayers and supplications, with loud cries and tears, to the one who was able to save him from death, and he was heard because of his reverent submission. [8] Although he was a Son, he learned obedience through what he suffered; [9] and having been made perfect, he became the source of eternal salvation for all who obey him, [10] having been designated by God a high priest according to the order of Melchizedek.

Initial Observations

Theses two passages are probably the best known and best loved from the Letter to the Hebrews. The letter as a whole is a highly sophisticated document, with a somewhat tortuous style. The author alternates between reflection on the Christ event, seen through the lens of the Temple, and exhortation, presented as practical advice.

The distinctive rhetorical character of Hebrews is evident in the introduction (1:1–4), which sets the tone in both content and rhetorical power for the remainder of the homily. The author demonstrates the ultimacy of the Christian revelation in comparison with God's previous disclosures in the Old Testament (1:1–2), and develops the high Christological claim with the rhetorical device of comparison ('greater than'; cf. Hebrews 6:9; 7:7, 19, 22; 8:6; 11:16, 40; 12:24). Because of the exaltation to God's right hand (Psalm 110:1), Christ is greater than all counterparts from the Old Testament.

Kind of writing

It has been wittily said that St Paul's Letter to the Hebrews is *not* by St Paul, is *not* a letter and is *not* addressed to the Hebrews! Our title for this document is a later addition in the manuscript tradition.

Although Hebrews contains an epistolary conclusion (13:18–25), the remainder of the book has a totally different character from the Christian epistolary tradition that began with Paul. It lacks the epistolary opening, the common epistolary topics, and the argumentative structure of the Pauline Epistles. Indeed, the author refers to his message as a 'word of exhortation' (Hebrews 13:22), a term that is used elsewhere (Acts 13:15) for a synagogue sermon. This was a rhetorical form that had developed in the Hellenistic Jewish synagogue consisting of 1) an indicative or exemplary section in the form of scripture quotations or theological points; 2) a conclusion based on the exemplary section; and 3) an exhortation to the community. Unlike the Pauline Epistles, Hebrews follows the common pattern of the word of exhortation. The epistolary conclusion is added to the homily because the author's sermon had to be sent around.

Old Testament background

The key text behind all of Hebrews is Psalm 110:

> The Lord says to my lord, 'Sit at my right hand until I make your enemies your footstool.' The Lord sends out from Zion your mighty sceptre. Rule in the midst of your foes. Your people will offer themselves willingly on the day you lead your forces on the holy mountains. From the womb of the morning, like dew, your youth will come to you. The Lord has sworn and will not change his mind, 'You are a priest forever according to the order of Melchizedek.' The Lord is at your right hand; he will shatter kings on the day of his wrath. He will execute judgment among the nations, filling them with corpses; he will shatter heads over the wide earth. He will drink from the stream by the path; therefore he will lift up his head. (Psalm 110:1–7)

Melchizedek is a somewhat mysterious figure in the Bible. The unique narrative mention in Genesis 14, with its many 'gaps' in the telling, triggered a great deal of later speculation.

After his return from the defeat of Chedorlaomer and the kings who were with him, the king of Sodom went out to meet him at the Valley of Shaveh (that is, the King's Valley). And King Melchizedek of Salem brought out bread and wine; he was priest of God Most High. He blessed him and said, 'Blessed be Abram by God Most High, maker of heaven and earth; and blessed be God Most High, who has delivered your enemies into your hand!' And Abram gave him one tenth of everything. Then the king of Sodom said to Abram, 'Give me the persons, but take the goods for yourself.' But Abram said to the king of Sodom, 'I have sworn to the Lord, God Most High, maker of heaven and earth, that I would not take a thread or a sandal-thong or anything that is yours, so that you might not say, "I have made Abram rich." I will take nothing but what the young men have eaten, and the share of the men who went with me – Aner, Eshcol and Mamre. Let them take their share.' (Genesis 14:17–24)

New Testament foreground

Temple symbolism is important in the Gospels and in Paul. 'Do you not know that you are God's temple and that God's Spirit dwells in you? If anyone destroys God's temple, God will destroy that person. For God's temple is holy, and you are that temple.' (1 Corinthians 3:16–17)

St Paul

For all who rely on the works of the law are under a curse; for it is written, 'Cursed is everyone who does not observe and obey all the things written in the book of the law.' Now it is evident that no one is justified before God by the law; for 'The one who is righteous will live by faith.' But the law does not rest on faith; on the contrary, 'Whoever does the works of the law will live by them.' Christ redeemed us from the curse of the law by becoming a curse for us – for it is written, 'Cursed is everyone who hangs on a tree'— in order

that in Christ Jesus the blessing of Abraham might come
to the Gentiles, so that we might receive the promise of the
Spirit through faith. (Galatians 3:10–14)

Brief Commentary

(V. 14)
This is an exhortation, starting in 14 and concluding in 16. The readers
already believe Jesus is the Son of God. The high priest enjoyed a
representative role. 'Passed through' referred originally to the high priest
entering the Holy of Holies, but here Jesus enters the real sanctuary,
heaven, symbolised by the earthly Temple.

(V. 15)
This is the topic of the letter: Jesus' priesthood is through the unexpected
step of compassionate solidarity with sinners – like us is every respect
– not by means of sacred separation, as in the biblical tradition. In
Hebrews, we also find information on the treatment of Christians
(friction with society, abuse, imprisonment).

(V. 16)
The grace (= gift, literally) is underlined twice, so that we need have no
hesitation coming to this intermediary, who has achieved his priestly
office in his death and resurrection, assuring us of the mercy and help
we need.

(V. 7)
The full section here would be 5:5–10. Jesus' offering was similar (prayers
and supplications) and different (reverent submission by the Son of
God). His prayer to be delivered from death is on one level not heard
and at another level heard for the benefit of us all. Out (*ek* in Greek)
can mean 'from' and 'out of'. He prayed to be saved *from* death and God
saved him (and us) *out of* (= by means of) death.

(V. 8)
This verse is difficult theologically. Although Jesus was never disobedient
to God, he could not demonstrate obedience until he was placed in

situations where the will of God was challenged and obedience was required. There was constancy in Jesus' unfailing obedience to God's will, yet, as he encountered new situations, his faithfulness to God was challenged and his obedience was shaped accordingly.

(V. 9)

Jesus was perfected – as a human being before God and as a priest – and therefore exalted as the fulfilment of the Temple service. Suffering does not negate salvation, but is the way by which God brings about salvation.

(V.10)

Melchizedek is a mysterious figure about which there was much speculation at the time of Jesus. He is used in Hebrews for several reasons. (i) He predates the Levitical priesthood, which permits the author to say Jesus was a priest although not a descendant of Levi. (ii) 'Without father, without mother, without genealogy, having neither beginning of days nor end of life, but resembling the Son of God, he remains a priest forever.' (Hebrews 7:3) Jesus, as the Son of God, is 'without genealogy, without beginning of days' and is resurrected from the dead (without end).

Pointers for prayer

a) One of the greatest blocks in a relationship is when you meet with a person who is unable to sympathise with where you are. Think of the difference it has made to you when you met someone who was able to tune in to your experience of difficulties, worry or pain. What does it mean to you to think of Jesus as one able to sympathise with you in all your weaknesses?

b) The author encourages us to 'approach the throne of grace with boldness'. Can you recall times when your trust in another enabled you to approach that person with confidence in a time of need with the result that you 'received mercy' and 'found grace'? What has encouraged and built up your confidence to approach God, or Jesus, in that way?

c) Life can be a harsh teacher, and for none more so than for Jesus. He suffered for his unwavering trust in God. His 'reverent submission', his 'obedience' in the face of unbelievable suffering and opposition enhance the credibility of his testimony. He lived what he said. What people have you known that you trusted because you knew just how they had been tested and stood firm? Have there been times when your words have been given added power because you spoke from lived experience?

d) It was through the fidelity of Jesus to the mission given him by God that he became the source of eternal salvation for others. Have you ever found that your ability to cope with reality enables you to help others? Or have you found that when you can draw on your faith and trust in God to help you in difficult circumstances, then you can also be a source of 'salvation', or help, for others?

Prayer

Lord God, whose compassion embraces all peoples, whose law is wisdom, freedom, and joy for the poor, fulfil in our midst your promise of favour, that we may receive the gospel of salvation with faith and, anointed by the Spirit, freely proclaim it. Through Christ our Lord. Amen.

🌿 First Reading 🌿

Is 52:13 See, my servant shall prosper; he shall be exalted and lifted up, and shall be very high. [14] Just as there were many who were astonished at him – so marred was his appearance, beyond human semblance, and his form beyond that of mortals – [15] so he shall startle many nations; kings shall shut their mouths because of him; for that which had not been told them they shall see, and that which they had not heard they shall contemplate.

Is 53:1 Who has believed what we have heard? And to whom has the arm of the LORD been revealed? ² For he grew up before him like a young plant, and like a root out of dry ground; he had no form or majesty that we should look at him, nothing in his appearance that we should desire him. ³ He was despised and rejected by others; a man of suffering and acquainted with infirmity; and as one from whom others hide their faces he was despised, and we held him of no account.

Is 53:4 Surely he has borne our infirmities and carried our diseases; yet we accounted him stricken, struck down by God, and afflicted. ⁵ But he was wounded for our transgressions, crushed for our iniquities; upon him was the punishment that made us whole, and by his bruises we are healed. ⁶ All we like sheep have gone astray; we have all turned to our own way, and the LORD has laid on him the iniquity of us all.

Is 53:7 He was oppressed, and he was afflicted, yet he did not open his mouth; like a lamb that is led to the slaughter, and like a sheep that before its shearers is silent, so he did not open his mouth. ⁸ By a perversion of justice he was taken away. Who could have imagined his future? For he was cut off from the land of the living, stricken for the transgression of my people. ⁹ They made his grave with the wicked and his tomb with the rich, although he had done no violence, and there was no deceit in his mouth.

Is 53:10 Yet it was the will of the LORD to crush him with pain. When you make his life an offering for sin, he shall see his offspring, and shall prolong his days; through him the will of the LORD shall prosper. ¹¹ Out of his anguish he shall see light; he shall find satisfaction through his knowledge. The righteous one, my servant, shall make many righteous, and he shall bear their iniquities. ¹² Therefore I will allot him a portion with the great, and he shall divide the spoil with the strong; because he poured out himself to death, and was numbered with the transgressors; yet he bore the sin of many, and made intercession for the transgressors.

Initial Observations

In Second Isaiah (40–55), God's help to Israel is expressed in three ways: creation/redemption, the vindication of the Servant and the return to Zion. In particular, there are four Suffering Servant Songs (42:1–4; 49:1–6; 50:4–11 and 52:13–53:12), identified by later scholarship. Scholars have struggled to establish the meaning at the time of writing and Jewish readings note the parallel with the ministry of Jeremiah (Jeremiah 10:18–24; 11:19) and similarities with other texts in Isaiah. At the same time, these poems have proved an especially rich resource for early Christian reflection on the cross. Today's passage is the longest and most striking of the four.

Kind of writing

This passage is a poem, displaying the common features of biblical poetry: Old Testament reference, metaphors and parallelism (i.e. two lines saying the same thing in different words [synonymous]). Isaiah 53:1–9 illustrates the parallelism very clearly. As for the typical language, cf. Psalm 18:5–6, 30:4; Psalm 91:15–16; Jonah 2:2, 8; Isaiah 2:12–14; 5:1–6; 11:1–10.

Origin of the reading

The reading comes from Second Isaiah, that is Isaiah 40–55, written during the Babylonian exile. In some fashion, the 'servant' models the interiorisation of suffering for the sake of the community.

Related passages

In the first poem (Isaiah 42:1–4 [5–9]), the Lord describes his servant as chosen, endowed with the Spirit, humble and compassionate. He will persevere until he brings justice to the nations. In the second poem the servant testifies that he is called before birth, prepared as Yahweh's special, hidden weapon; the servant feels that his labour is in vain, yet he will trust in God to vindicate him (Isaiah 49:1–4).

In the third poem poem, Israel is identified as the servant (Isaiah 49:3), whose mission, paradoxically, is to restore fallen Israel and to be a light to the nations (49:5–7). Although the term 'servant' is missing from Isaiah 50:4–9 [10–11], most scholars consider this passage to be part of the series. Here the servant is the Lord's faithful, obedient disciple, enduring scorn, abuse and painful beatings, yet continuing to trust in God to vindicate him.

In the fourth poem (Isaiah 52:13—53:12) a group, probably the nations, speaks of the servant's vicarious sufferings on their behalf and of his ultimate exaltation. There is a wide discussion of the identity of the servant and those who speak for him.

Brief commentary

(V. 13)
Cf. Isaiah 42:1–4. The poem begins with exaltation from God (cf. Isaiah 49:7).

(V. 14ff.)
The humiliation is expressed through its effects on others; suffering disfigures (cf. Psalm 8:5) and frightens.

(V. 1)
A 'chorus' speaks ('we'), probably Israel. The Lord's presence is difficult to discern, even though the action and message confirm each other mutually.

(V. 2f.)
A biography starts: 2 (birth and maturation); 3 and 7 (suffering and passion); 8 (execution and death); 9 (burial); 10–11a (glorification). Who exactly this person is remains mysterious (cf. Psalm 31:11ff.; 38:8, 9, 12; Lamentations 3:1, 14). 'Root' and 'majesty' hint at Davidic status, perhaps even Messianic identity.

(V. 4f.)

Here it is not the victim but the spectators who confess their sins. Initially, following biblical teaching, they interpret the suffering as punishment. The chorus expresses the paradox of suffering which healed (cf. 1 Peter 2:22–25).

(V. 6)

A classical image of sin (gone astray), which prepares us for v. 7.

(V. 7)

The silence of the servant is directly mentioned – cf. Job 3!

(V. 8)

Unjust condemnation – Psalm 7:7, 9, 12; 35:11, 23, 24. In contrast, this servant does not lament the injustice of his suffering (cf. Habakkuk 1:12–17).

(V. 9)

This verse points to the common grave of criminals.

(V. 10f.)

The shock here is that the humiliation was complete, without relief or apparent vindication. Expiation – a term to have a big history in Christianity – is unique in Isaiah, but cf. Leviticus 4–5; 7; 14; 19. Precisely because of the few references in Isaiah, it is difficult to interpret. A light dawns as a symbol of reversal and salvation.

(V. 12)

God confirms his promise given at the start of the poem, declaring null the human exercise of justice. Somehow, this innocent suffering brings salvation to the many (cf. Luke 22:37).

Pointers for prayer

a) This Song of the Suffering Servant, originally referring to the Jewish nation, applies very aptly to Jesus. As you read it, how does it highlight for you the love God has shown us in Jesus?

b) There have also been people in more recent times who have been suffering servants and whose suffering has been a source of life for others: Gandhi, Martin Luther King, Oscar Romero, Nelson Mandela and others. Whose lives have spoken to you in this way?

c) The story of any long-term helpful and life-giving relationship may have moments with an echo of the Suffering Servant theme. Who has been a suffering servant for you, through whose sufferings have you been healed? For whom have you shown that kind of love?

d) One can also use this passage as a way of understanding the personal experience of coming face to face with the shadow side of ourselves. Have you ever been 'appalled' at what you have seen in yourself? Have you felt you were 'disfigured', 'without beauty', 'a thing despised'? Did you want to 'screen your face' from what you saw? Yet have there been occasions when, by painfully and patiently facing the truth of what you saw, the experience turned out to be a 'punishment that brings peace' and by your wounds you were healed?

Prayer

Be mindful, Lord, of this your family, for whose sake our Lord Jesus Christ, when betrayed, did not hesitate to yield himself into his enemies' hands and undergo the agony of the cross. Who lives and reigns with you in the unity of the Holy Spirit, God for ever and ever. Amen.

Chapter 9

Easter Vigil A

Thought for the day

Tonight we proclaim the creator God, the God of life, who gives life, who is always faithful and who raised Jesus from the dead. Christ is risen, he is truly risen! But, in a forthright way, what difference does it make? If it is true that Christ is risen and that to God all are alive and that our present relationship with God will withstand the destruction of death, that is, if it is true that this very night we are radically set free from the power of death and even the fear of death, then, everything is utterly different. Suddenly, we are free, free to a bewildering degree — free to love, free to serve without counting the cost, free to live without fear, free to embrace the whole adventure of life, free to give ourselves to God, free even to die. For freedom Christ has set us free. (Galatians 5:1)

Prayer

Tonight, we come before you, God of the living, filled with wonder, and we shout again our alleluia! Alleluia, for your faithfulness in Christ. Alleluia, for his resurrection. Alleluia, for our new life in Christ. Alleluia, for the promise of deliverance from sin and death. May we embrace the freedom we have in Christ and have the courage to live it in lives of loving service. Through the same Christ our Lord. Amen.

🌿 Gospel 🌿

Mt 28:1 After the sabbath, as the first day of the week was dawning, Mary Magdalene and the other Mary went to see the tomb. [2] And suddenly there was a great earthquake; for an angel of the Lord, descending from heaven, came and rolled back the stone and sat on it. [3] His appearance was like lightning, and his clothing white as snow. [4] For fear of him the guards shook and became like dead men. [5] But the angel said to the women, 'Do not be afraid; I know that you are looking for Jesus who was crucified. [6] He is not here; for he has been raised, as he said. Come, see the place where he lay. [7] Then go quickly and tell his disciples, "He has been raised from the dead, and indeed he is going ahead of you to Galilee; there you will see him."'This is my message for you.' [8] So they left the tomb quickly with fear and great joy, and ran to tell his disciples. [9] Suddenly Jesus met them and said, 'Greetings!' And they came to him, took hold of his feet, and worshipped him. [10] Then Jesus said to them, 'Do not be afraid; go and tell my brothers to go to Galilee; there they will see me.'

Initial observations

We distinguish 'empty tomb proclamation narratives' and 'resurrection appearance narratives'. In all four Gospels, there are empty tomb proclamation narratives. Mark lacks any resurrection appearance narrative; the other Gospels have a variety of stories, but they do not repeat or confirm each other. There is, however, a historical core that all the accounts share: the first day of the week, early, women, divine figure(s), empty tomb, reassurance, a proclamation. After that each set of stories has a different angle on the events, exploring different dimensions. In Matthew, we catch a glimpse of the construction of a resurrection appearance narrative based on the empty tomb proclamation narrative. Again in Matthew, the apologetic aspect is to the fore, as may be seen from the unique story of the guards.

Kind of writing

(i) The content of the story is, by definition, unique. However, the literary form is recognisably that of 'epiphany', i.e. an encounter with the divine, the transcendent (symbolised here by earthquake, angel, descent, heaven, lighting, clothing). Classically, religious experience shows these features: (i) the encounter is unexpected; (ii) the participants experience awe and dread – in our version this is called 'fear'; (iii) the message from the divine figure(s) is 'Do not be afraid'.

(ii) In these verses there are two epiphanies, one very like the other. The first is an 'empty tomb proclamation narrative' and the other is a 'resurrection appearance narrative'. It might be argued that the second epiphany is a making explicit, in somewhat less metaphorical language, of the content of the first epiphany.

There are two sets of interesting parallels here, which may help us to recognise what kind of writing this is. The first is a parallel in religious symbolism between the death and resurrection:

Matthew 27:51-54	Matthew 28:1-4
Mt 27:51 At that moment the curtain of the temple was torn in two, from top to bottom. The earth shook, and the rocks were split. [52] The tombs also were opened, and many bodies of the saints who had fallen asleep were raised. [53] After his resurrection they came out of the tombs and entered the holy city and appeared to many. [54] Now when the centurion and those with him, who were keeping watch over Jesus, saw the earthquake and what took place, they were terrified and said, 'Truly this man was God's Son!'	**Mt 28:2** And suddenly there was a great earthquake; for an angel of the Lord, descending from heaven, came and rolled back the stone and sat on it. [3] His appearance was like lightning, and his clothing white as snow. [4] For fear of him the guards shook and became like dead men.

The second parallel is between the appearance and words of the angel and the appearance and words of the Risen Lord.

Matthew 28:1-8	Matthew 28:9-10
Mt 28:2 And suddenly there was a great earthquake; for an angel of the Lord, descending from heaven, came and rolled back the stone and sat on it. **Mt 28:5** But the angel said to the women, 'Do not be afraid; I know that you are looking for Jesus who was crucified. **Mt 28:7** Then go quickly and tell his disciples, "He has been raised from the dead, and indeed he is going ahead of you to Galilee; there you will see him." This is my message for you.'	**Mt 28:9** Suddenly Jesus met them and said, 'Greetings!' And they came to him, took hold of his feet, and worshipped him. [10] Then Jesus said to them, 'Do not be afraid; go and tell my brothers to go to Galilee; there they will see me.'

An appearance of the Risen Lord at the empty tomb is found only in Matthew in the Synoptic gospels. It looks as if the gospel writer was unhappy to leave the implied encounter with the Risen One implicit and went on to make it explicit.

Old Testament background

(i)Resurrection, in the sense of a genuinely personal afterlife, is not mentioned in the Bible until we come to the books of Daniel and 1 and 2 Maccabees. It is mentioned metaphorically in Ezekiel, when he tells the exiles that a future generation will arise and will return to the land of Israel. That said, across the Old Testament generally, death is not a problem – just the natural next stage, as long as you (a) have children and (b) do not die prematurely.

(ii)The development of resurrection faith was triggered by the experience of martyrdom. It is a teaching of the Old Testament that God, eventually, rewards the just and punishes the wicked, even if this is not always obvious. But in the case of those who have been faithful to the point of death, when could God reward them unless there were some life after death?

The OT background to resurrection, foreshadowed in Isaiah 25:6–10 and Ezekiel 37, is found in only two biblical books: Daniel and 2 Maccabees. The third text below is from the Dead Sea Scrolls (Qumran), a unique text linking resurrection with the Messiah. Gaps in this defective manuscript are indicated by three dots.

'At that time Michael, the great prince, the protector of your people, shall arise. There shall be a time of anguish, such as has never occurred since nations first came into existence. But at that time your people shall be delivered, everyone who is found written in the book. Many of those who sleep in the dust of the earth shall awake, some to everlasting life, and some to shame and everlasting contempt. Those who are wise shall shine like the brightness of the sky, and those who lead many to righteousness, like the stars for ever and ever. But you, Daniel, keep the words secret and the book sealed until the time of the end. Many shall be running back and forth, and evil shall increase.' (Daniel 12:1–4)

The mother was especially admirable and worthy of honourable memory. Although she saw her seven sons perish within a single day, she bore it with good courage because of her hope in the Lord. She encouraged each of them in the language of their ancestors. Filled with a noble spirit, she reinforced her woman's reasoning with a man's courage, and said to them, 'I do not know how you came into being in my womb. It was not I who gave you life and breath, nor I who set in order the elements within each of you. Therefore the Creator of the world, who shaped the beginning of humankind and devised the origin of all things, will in his mercy give life and breath back to you again, since you now forget yourselves for the sake of his laws.' (2 Maccabees 7:20–23)

… For the heavens and the earth shall listen to *His Messiah* and all which is in them shall not turn away from the commandments of the holy ones. Strengthen yourselves, O you who seek the Lord, in His service. Will you not find the Lord in this, all those who hope in their heart? For the Lord attends to the pious and calls the righteous by name. Over the humble His spirit hovers, and He renews the faithful in His strength. For He will honour the pious upon the throne of His eternal kingdom, setting prisoners free, opening the eyes of the blind, raising up those who are bowed down (Psalm 146:7–8).

And for ever I shall hold fast to those who hope and in His faithfulness shall ... and the fruit of good deeds shall not be delayed for anyone and the Lord shall do glorious things which have not been done, just as He said. For He shall heal the critically wounded, *He shall revive the dead*, He shall send good news to the afflicted (Isaiah 61:1),

He shall satisfy the poor, He shall guide the uprooted, He shall make the hungry rich, and ... discerning ones ... and all of them as the holy ones ... and ... (4Q Messianic Apocalypse f2ii+4:1–15).

New Testament foreground

(i) The Passion Predictions include the hope of resurrection (Matthew 16:21; 17:22; 20:17–19).

(ii) Jesus' own teaching of the resurrection may be found in Matthew 22:23–33.

(iii) Matthew has a substantial apologetic interest, as is evident from the story about the guards which follows. (The guards' story is quite improbable historically. Henry Wansbrough speaks of 'the transparent idiocy' of the excuse given by the guards.) This apologetic interest affects his burial scene, his tomb appearance and also provides an insertion between the appearance story and the commission story. His other great interest is the church. Matthew seems to be dealing with an established community, which has a certain structure (see Matthew 16:19 and 18:18). This is the context for the last resurrection scene in Matthew, which includes a promise to be 'with you always, to the end of the age'.

St Paul

We know that Christ, being raised from the dead, will never die again; death no longer has dominion over him. The death he died, he died to sin, once for all; but the life he lives, he lives to God. So you also must consider yourselves dead to sin and alive to God in Christ Jesus. (Romans 6:9–11)

For I handed on to you as of first importance what I in turn had received: that Christ died for our sins in accordance with the scriptures, and that he was buried, and that he was raised on the third day in accordance with the scriptures, and that he appeared to Cephas, then to the twelve. Then he appeared to more than five hundred brothers and sisters at one time, most of whom are still alive, though some have died. Then he appeared to James, then to all the apostles. Last of all, as to one untimely born, he appeared also to me. For I am the least of the apostles, unfit to be called an apostle, because I persecuted the church of God. But by the grace of God I am what I am, and his grace towards me has not been in vain. On the contrary, I worked harder than any of them – though it was not I, but the grace of God that is with me. Whether then it was I or they, so we proclaim and so you have come to believe. (1 Corinthians 15:3–11)

Brief commentary

(V.1)

In Mark, three women buy spices on Saturday night and on Sunday come to anoint the body. All those details are missing in Matthew: two women come to the tomb, apparently to mourn ('to see the tomb'), with no thought of entering (cf. Matthew 27:58, 61).

(V. 2)

The earthquake is an addition of Matthew – he introduces three earthquakes into his Gospel, making him something of a seismophiliac. An earthquake is a biblical metaphor of God's presence and action. An 'angel' is a symbolic figure, again signifying the transcendent (Mark, a young man in white; Matthew, an angel like lightning, outside; Luke, two men in dazzling clothes; John, two angels in white, inside). Precision does not matter here – the key is the symbolic function of these apocalyptic 'props'.

(V. 3)

Lightning is one of the end-time symbols in Matthew and in Revelation (Matthew 24:27; 28:3; Revelation 4:5; 8:5; 11:19; 16:18). The same could be said of the snow (Matthew 28:3; Revelation 1:14). White is the colour of heavenly garments. This is the nearest any of the canonical Gospels come to describing the resurrection. (There is a description the non-canonical Gospel of Peter, 9:34–10:42.)

(V. 4)

This is found in Matthew only because of his apologetic interest in the guards. The reaction of fear belongs to the epiphany genre.

(V. 5)

The reassurance is likewise part of the genre of an epiphany or theophany. Carefully, the risen one is identified with the crucified one – possibly against those who disregard the importance of the cross in Christian faith.

(V. 6)

The empty tomb – the empirical residue of the resurrection so to speak – corroborates the proclamation rather than vice versa.

(V. 7)

Authentic epiphanies include a mission and the women are given a message to proclaim. As there are no resurrection appearance narratives in Galilee, apart from the great commission, the reference is puzzling. It could be that Matthew is thinking that towards the end of a brief mission to the Gentiles (Galilee), they would meet the Lord in the Second Coming, rather like Mark (cf. Matthew 26:32 and the fulfilment in Matthew 28:16–20).

(V. 8)

Matthew discreetly converts the silence of the women in Mark ('they said nothing to anyone, for they were afraid') into 'great joy'. Matthew, with a future church structure, has no place for the abject failure of the disciples (a theme of Mark). Clearly, the women did not stay silent *for ever*!

(Vv. 9–10)

This encounter unfolds the symbolic meaning of the previous one. The message is identical and the only addition is the making explicit of the person of Jesus. The reaction describes the *mysterium tremendum*.

Pointers for prayer

a) The identity of Jesus is revealed as the Messiah and the Son of God, not with a display of human power, but as one who was prepared to suffer unto death to show us how our God loves us. How does the Passion story speak to you as a revelation of how God loves you?

b) We are dealing here with an encounter with the divine, characterised thus: (i) the encounter is unexpected; (ii) the participants experience awe and dread; (iii) the message from the divine figure(s) is 'do not be afraid'. When have you had some kind of an encounter with the divine?

c) The women had just experienced the trauma of the crucifixion, an event that spoke of death and not life. What had happened took on a totally different significance in the light of the resurrection. It spoke of life rather than death. When have you received a message of hope and life in a time of pain or discouragement?

d) 'Do not be afraid' is one of the most repeated phrases in the Gospels. Who have been the 'angels' who have helped to calm you and take away fear? For whom have you been able to do this?

e) The women were told to go and convey the message they had received to others. What is your experience of being a messenger of good news to others, whether trivial or significant? Does past experience come back to you?

Prayer

O God, your saving plan has brought us to the glory of this night.

Slaves, we become your sons and daughters, poor, your mercy makes us rich, sinners, you count us among your saints.

Bring us to know the place that is ours in the unfolding story of your purpose, and instil in our hearts the wonder of your salvation.

Grant this through Jesus Christ, our Passover and our peace, who lives and reigns with you now and always in the unity of the Holy Spirit, God for ever and ever. Amen.

🌿 New Testament Reading 🌿

Rom 6:3 Do you not know that all of us who have been baptised into Christ Jesus were baptised into his death? ⁴ Therefore we have been buried with him by baptism into death, so that, just as Christ was raised from the dead by the glory of the Father, so we too might walk in newness of life.

Rom 6:5 For if we have been united with him in a death like his, we will certainly be united with him in a resurrection like his. ⁶ We know that our old self was crucified with him so that the body of sin might be destroyed, and we might no longer be enslaved to sin. ⁷ For whoever has died is freed from sin. ⁸ But if we have died with Christ, we believe that we will also live with him. [9] We know that Christ, being raised from the dead, will never die again; death no longer has dominion over him. [10] The death he died, he died to sin, once for all; but the life he lives, he lives to God. [11] So you also must consider yourselves dead to sin and alive to God in Christ Jesus.

Initial observations

In the course of Romans 5–8, Paul gives a very comprehensive account of all that the Roman Christians – both Jews and Gentiles – have received from Christ. It makes for remarkable reading and not least his account of baptism in chapter 6. His hope is that with so much in common, the Roman Christians will be able to overcome their differences in the light of all they have received.

Kind of writing

In the letter, Paul argues from many angles. At this point, he is trying to get the Roman Christians to register in their minds all they have received and, he hopes, in light of that, that they may be able to set aside their differences.

Context in the community

No one knows who founded the Roman churches – certainly not Paul. As noted in the Initial Observations, the community split along Jewish and Gentile lines. The presenting issue was how much of the received Jewish tradition should be insisted upon. What happened in Rome mattered to Paul because it touched the heart of his Gospel – the reconciliation of Jew and Gentile in Christ – and because it was happening in the capital city of the Roman Empire.

Related passages

In the same way, my friends, you have died to the law through the body of Christ, so that you may belong to another, to him who has been raised from the dead in order that we may bear fruit for God. While we were living in the flesh, our sinful passions, aroused by the law, were at work in our members to bear fruit for death. But now we are discharged from the law, dead to that which held us captive, so that we are slaves not under the old written code but in the new life of the Spirit. (Romans 7:4–6)

For the love of Christ urges us on, because we are convinced that one has died for all; therefore all have died. And he died for all, so that those who live might live no longer for themselves, but for him who died and was raised for them. (2 Corinthians 5:14–15)

Brief commentary

(V. 3)
Paul is arguing here from their experience and a good interpretation of it.

(V. 4)
Paul evokes the symbolism of immersion and draws consequences for the way we live in *newness of life.*

(V. 5)
This is our Christian hope, the hope of transformations, which begins now in our inner selves and in our way of living.

(Vv. 6–7)
Paul implies that the behaviour of judging our neighbour is evidence that we are not yet set free.

(V. 8)
The alarming information that we 'have died' is echoed later in Colossians 3:1–4.

(Vv. 9–10)
Christ is now free from death and has conquered sin. *Therefore,* the life he

lives he lives to God (an apocalyptic expression). There are consequences for us today, as we see in the very next verse.

(V. 11)
And, therefore, we too *ought* to be radically new and transformed in our lives and manner of treating others. Given all we have received – life, forgiveness and hope – we simply *should* to be living transformed lives.

Pointers for prayer

a) As most of us were baptised as infants, we have to make an effort to recover the power of baptism and its meaning for us. What has helped you recognise your dignity as Christian baptised into Christ?

b) Paul has a strong sense of truly being set free and he believes 'yes, we can' lead a new a full life in Christ now in the present moment. It is always a challenge!

Prayer

As we recall our baptism on this very night, help us embrace our new life in Christ that we may be his followers in name and in fact.
Through Christ our Lord. Amen.

Old Testament Vigil Readings

For the Vigil Readings, a very brief introduction is provided, as well as some historical contextualisation and related New Testament texts, either for personal reflection or liturgical use.

Reading 1: Genesis 1:1–2:2

Our contemporary wonder at the universe was shared by the ancient writer who composed this poetic account of creation. All God made is good, even very good!

Historical Note
Written probably during or after the Babylonian Exile (587–39 BC)

Related New Testament Passages

In the beginning was the Word, and the Word was with God, and the Word was God. He was in the beginning with God. All things came into being through him, and without him not one thing came into being. What has come into being in him was life, and the life was the light of all people. The light shines in the darkness, and the darkness did not overcome it. (John 1:1–5)

For it is the God who said, 'Let light shine out of darkness,' who has shone in our hearts to give the light of the knowledge of the glory of God in the face of Jesus Christ. (2 Corinthians 4:6)

Reading 2: Genesis 22:1–18

What could be behind this reading? Perhaps the experience that trusting in God sometimes feels 'counter-intuitive'. For all its difficulty, Abraham comes across as our father in faith.

Historical Note

Originally, it may have been a cult legend against child sacrifice. As it stands now in the Bible, the story is the tenth of the ten testings of Abraham, the man of faith.

Related New Testament Passages

For God so loved the world that he gave his only Son, so that everyone who believes in him may not perish but may have eternal life. (John 3:16)

For this reason it depends on faith, in order that the promise may rest on grace and be guaranteed to all his descendants, not only to the adherents of the law but also to those who share the faith of Abraham (for he is the father of all of us, as it is written, 'I have made you the father of many nations') – in the presence of the God in whom he believed, who gives life to the dead and calls into existence the things that do not exist. (Romans 4:16–17)

Reading 3: Exodus 14:15 – 5:1

This story of liberation – even with its disturbing dimensions – dramatically portrays God as a God of liberation. This reading has inspired people over the centuries, especially the oppressed, because our God desires us to be free.

Historical Note
Behind our text there may well be an ancient memory of a slave escape, written up theatrically, perhaps during the Babylonian Exile. It became the foundation myth of the Israelites (myth in the strong sense!!).

Related New TestamentPassages
> For our paschal lamb, Christ, has been sacrificed. (1 Corinthians 5:7)

> Were you a slave when called? Do not be concerned about it. Even if you can gain your freedom, make use of your present condition now more than ever. For whoever was called in the Lord as a slave is a freed person belonging to the Lord, just as whoever was free when called is a slave of Christ. (1 Corinthians 7:21–22)

Reading 4: Isaiah 54:5–14

Using the experience and metaphor of married love, the reading offers a rich exploration of God's constancy, God's faithful love to Israel and to us all.

Historical Note
Probably written during the Babylonian Exile, when people felt God had abandoned them.

Related New Testament Passages
> Let us rejoice and exult and give him the glory, for the marriage of the Lamb has come, and his bride has made herself ready; to her it has been granted to be clothed with fine linen, bright and pure'– for the fine linen is the righteous deeds of the saints. And the angel said to me, 'Write this:

Blessed are those who are invited to the marriage supper of the Lamb.' (Revelation 19:7–9)

Reading 5: Isaiah 55:1–11

We thirst for God and, in a strange way, God thirsts for us.

Historical Note

Written just after the return from exile in Babylon, during a period of faltering reconstruction. The message is clear: God's word achieves what it sets out to do.

Related New Testament Passages

On the last day of the festival, the great day, while Jesus was standing there, he cried out, 'Let anyone who is thirsty come to me, and let the one who believes in me drink. As the scripture has said, "Out of his heart shall flow rivers of living water."' Now he said this about the Spirit, which believers in him were to receive; for as yet there was no Spirit, because Jesus was not yet glorified. (John 7:37–39)

And the Word became flesh and lived among us, and we have seen his glory, the glory as of a father's only son, full of grace and truth. (John 1:14)

Reading 6: Baruch 3:9-15, 32-4:4

A wise person is a great friend to have … and what is wisdom? This reading offers a challenging portrait.

Historical Note

Jeremiah had a secretary called Baruch but he is not likely to have been the author of this short book. The book is of uncertain date, probably written in the Diaspora. The message is: recognise your sin and return to God, the fountain of life and wisdom.

Related New Testament Passages

Then he said to me, 'It is done! I am the Alpha and the Omega, the beginning and the end. To the thirsty I will give water as a gift from the spring of the water of life.' (Revelation 21:6)

For Jews demand signs and Greeks desire wisdom, but we proclaim Christ crucified, a stumbling block to Jews and foolishness to Gentiles, but to those who are the called, both Jews and Greeks, Christ the power of God and the wisdom of God. For God's foolishness is wiser than human wisdom, and God's weakness is stronger than human strength. (1 Corinthians 1:22–25)

Reading 7: Ezekiel 36:16–28

Where do we find hope? Where to we find the springs of renewal? Our final reading was written when people had more or less given up.

Historical Note
Ezekiel worked during the Babylonian Exile: God herself will bring about a change of heart and give all new hope by a change of heart.

Related New Testament Passages
Jesus answered, 'Very truly, I tell you, no one can enter the kingdom of God without being born of water and Spirit. What is born of the flesh is flesh, and what is born of the Spirit is spirit. Do not be astonished that I said to you, "You must be born from above."' (John 3:5–8)

So then, brothers and sisters, we are debtors, not to the flesh, to live according to the flesh – for if you live according to the flesh, you will die; but if by the Spirit you put to death the deeds of the body, you will live. For all who are led by the Spirit of God are children of God. For you did not receive a spirit of slavery to fall back into fear, but you have received a spirit of adoption. When we cry, 'Abba! Father!' it is that very Spirit bearing witness with our spirit that we are children of God, and if children, then heirs, heirs of God and joint heirs with Christ – if, in fact, we suffer with him so that we may also be glorified with him. (Romans 8:12-17)

Soli Deo Gloria!

Study Bibles

A good study bible can be of immense help. Here are some outstanding examples.

Ecumenical Study Bibles

The HarperCollins Study Bible. Fully revised and updated. Harold W. Attridge (general editor) New York, NY: HarperCollins Publishers, 2006.

The text is the New Revised Standard Version. This edition is really useful and perhaps the best because of the extensive notes. Paying close attention to the notes alone would as good as a course of bible study.

The NET Bible. Full Notes Edition. Nashville, TN: Thomas Nelson, 2019.

The New English Translation (NET) *is a fresh version in modern English from the USA. The notes on the text pay attention primarily to the words, with an eye to both manuscripts and meanings. This might not be the only study bible to have, but the wealth of information on the basic text is just extraordinary. The layout on the page is quite original and helpful.*

The New Oxford Annotated Bible. Fifth edition, fully revised and expanded. Michael D. Coogan (editor), Marc Zvi Brettler, Carols A. Newsom and Pheme Perkins (associated editors). New York, NY: Oxford University Press USA, 2018.

Again, the base text is the New Revised Standard Version. *Apart from different editors and commentators, this edition differs from the* HarperCollins Study Bible *in that the introductions are extensive and the notes are somewhat less ample.*

Jewish Study Bibles

The Jewish Study Bible. Second Edition. Adela Berlin and Marc Zvi Brettler (editors), New York, NY: Oxford University Press USA, 2014.

This new edition uses the Jewish Publication Society translation, the Tanakh. *The introductions, notes and essays are all excellent. Christian users will benefit from a commentary rooted in Jewish faith and scholarship. This edition includes many essays on history and interpretation under various headings. In a word, buy it!*

The Jewish Annotated New Testament. Second edition, fully revised and expanded. Amy Jill Levine and Marc Zvi Brettler (editors), New York, NY: Oxford University Press USA, 2017.

The translation used is the New Revised Standard Version. *The introduction, notes and essays are all by Jewish scholars of the New Testament and Jewish Christian relations. A terrific amount of information from the perspective of contemporary and traditional Judaism is brought to bear on the text. The essays at the end of the volume form a comprehensive introduction to Jewish backgrounds and perspectives on the Christian tradition. The* Jewish Study Bible *and the* Jewish Annotated New Testament *should be on every bible reader's shelf.*

Catholic Study Bibles

Revised New Jerusalem Bible, Study Edition. Henry Wansbrough (editor), London: Darton, Longman and Todd, 2019.

This new edition would be ideal for someone beginning to go a little deeper into Scripture. The introductions to each book are engaging while the notes over each Psalm will be found to be helpful. The translation is in the tradition of the Jerusalem Bible, while the Psalms are taken from the Revised Grail Psalm.

The New Jerusalem Bible. Standard Edition. Henry Wansbrough (editor). London: Darton, Longman and Todd, 1985.

This edition of the Jerusalem Bible is still useful because it so rich in introductions, notes and cross-references. By comparison, the same material in the most recent edition, the Revised New Jerusalem Bible, is significantly reduced.

The Catholic Study Bible. Third edition. Donald Senior, John Collins and Mary Ann Getting (editors). New York: Oxford University Press USA, 2016.

The base text is the New American Bible Revised Edition. The introductory material is outstanding and notes are insightful and extensive. There is a focus on the Catholic use of the Bible (it includes the lectionary readings for example), but the whole tone is very ecumenical and open.

Biblical Index

The index follows the order of Old Testament books as found in Catholic Bibles; the chapter and verse numbering follows the NRSV.